BLACK DOVES SPEAK

HERODOTUS AND THE LANGUAGES OF BARBARIANS

Rosaria Vignolo Munson

CENTER FOR HELLENIC STUDIES
Trustees for Harvard University
Washington, DC
Distributed by Harvard University Press
Cambridge, Massachusetts, and London, England
2005

LIBRARY OF CONGRESS CATALOGING-IN-PUBLICATION DATA

Munson, Rosaria Vignolo.
Black doves speak : Herodotus and the languages of Barbarians / by Rosaria
  Vignolo Munson.
     p. cm. — (Hellenic Studies ; 9)
  Includes bibliographical references and index.
  ISBN 0-674-01790-0
1. Herodotus—Knowledge—Language and languages. 2. Language and
  languages. I. Author. II. Title. III. Series.
  D56.52.H45M86 2005
  938'.0072'02—dc22

                                                            2005010512

Hellenic Studies 9

BLACK DOVES SPEAK

To Stephe

TABLE OF CONTENTS

ACKNOWLEDGMENTS

My warmest thanks go to Gregory Nagy, Casey Dué, Alexander Hollmann, Ryan Hackney, Ivy Livingston, and the entire CHS publication team.

INTRODUCTION

As HERODOTUS EXPLORES HOW MUCH and in which ways human societies are mutually different, he takes for granted the generally recognized subdivision of the world into Greeks and barbarians.[1] But this common-view discourse provides only a partial framework of explanation for the text of the *Histories*.[2] The language of the Greek-barbarian antithesis stands in a dialogic relationship with a more complex and pluralistic opinion of the world.[3] This other voice never entirely silences the first, but it emerges as an insistent challenge in the flow of evidence throughout Herodotus' work.

Whether supported or not in any given context, the very notion of "barbarian" testifies to a criterion of difference that is to a great extent linguistic. Beyond any internal linguistic differentiation, Greek perception defines barbarian speech as anomalous and hard to understand.[4] The word *barbaros* itself may or may not have initially encoded the idea of indistinct or "funny" sound, though it eventually comes to do so.[5] Our earliest literary sources, at any rate, contain references to language (or languages) different

[1] The word *barbaros* occurs about 300 times in the *Histories*; see Powell 1938, s.v. Herodotus' uses are surveyed by Laurot 1981; see also Payen 1997.176.

[2] Cartledge 1993.356–362. Pelling 1997.

[3] In Bakhtinian terms, this prevalent, homogenizing, ideology would be "centripetal," in opposition to the "centrifugal" voice of dissent. Bakhtin 1981.270–308. The Bakhtinian notions of "dialogism" and "heteroglossia" in the novel have been applied to Herodotus by Pelling 2000.83, and to Homer by Peradotto 1990, esp. 53–58. For Bakhtin and the classics, see also the essays in Peradotto, et al. 1993 and Bracht Branham 2002.

[4] E.g. Sophocles *Ajax* 1262–1263. For other examples of "barbarian" as a generalized language (none in Herodotus), see Harrison 1998, ch. 3. "The Greek Conceptualization of Foreign Languages." For unintelligibility, see e.g. Plato *Protagoras* 341c, where Lesbian is said to be a "barbarian language" because hard to understand, and Thucydides 3.94.5 on the speech of the Eurytanes of Aetolia.

[5] Strabo 14.2.28. The term's possible Sumero-Babylonian derivation (Weidner 1913) does not preclude the onomatopeia *ba-ba*. Chantraine 1968–1980.164–165; Levy 1984; E. Hall 1989.4; Moggi 1991.36; Coleman 1997.178. But see the objections of J. Hall 1995 and 2002:111–112.

from that of the text even before they clearly formulate the notion of non-Greek in ethnic or cultural terms.[6] The *Iliad* identifies "foreign" with "foreign-speaking" when it calls the Carians *barbarophōnoi* (*Iliad* 2.867).[7] The leaders of these Carians, moreover, are said to be the sons of an individual, now dead, who "used to go to battle wearing gold, like a girl" (*Iliad* 2.872–873). This man is qualified as a fool, with a term that has a linguistic dimension: *nēpios* literally means 'infantile', like a baby who has not reached speaking age.[8]

Variations on this stereotype, which combines language difference with other negative features, become more pervasive and deliberate in later texts, especially with the politicization of the Greek-barbarian antithesis during and after the Persian Wars.[9] Foreign speech is almost invariably an index of primitivism, uncouthness, intellectual or cultural inferiority, irrationality, or madness.[10] Though all three tragedians make numerous references to the strangeness of foreign speech, Aeschylus has the greatest number in plays that have survived whole.[11] The *Persians* features exotic lamentations, the mention of Persian "noise," and catalogues of proper names that seek to capture the

[6] The *Iliad* refers to language difference only within the Trojan force (2.804; 4.436). Lejeune 1940–1948.52. Rotolo 1972.398. In the *Odyssey*, which displays a new preoccupation with cultural distinction between the "real world" of heroic epic and faraway lands, we find the epithets *allothrooi* (ἀλλόθροοι, 1.183, used by Athena/Mente of peoples to whose lands she has sailed; 3.302, of the Egyptians, where Menelaus traveled), and *agriophōnoi* (ἀγριόφωνοι, 8.294, of the Sinti of Lemnos). See also *Odyssey* 19.172–177 on the many languages (and dialects) spoken in Crete. *Homeric Hymn to Apollo* 3.162–169 mentions the existence of several *phōnai*, which could be either Greek dialects or foreign languages. *Homeric Hymn to Aphrodite* 5.113–114 mentions Trojan and Phrygian as languages different from one another and (presumably) from Greek.

[7] Werner 1989; Lejeune 1940–48.52; Levy 1984; Colvin 1999.41–50; J. Hall 2002.112. The Homeric epithet *barbarophōnoi* may mean "speaking bad Greek" (Strabo 14.2.28), but see Herodotus 8.135, where the Carian language is not apparently understood or recognized by Greek speakers. In other respects Herodotus (1.146, 171; 2.152, 154, 163; 3.11) and other sources agree in representing the Carians as culturally very similar to the Greeks.

[8] Cf. *Iliad* 3.237–238, where Nestor rebukes the Achaeans as being babies (νηπιάχοις) and speaking like children (παισὶν ἐοικότες ἀγοράασθε). On this passage, see Martin 1989.104.

[9] On the evolution of the Greek-barbarian polarity, see Diller 1961, esp. 39–68; Campos Daroca 1992.27–30; Cartledge 1993, esp. 36–62; Nippel 2002.279–293; Coleman 1997.186–194; J. Hall 1997.45–47; 2002.174–181; Rosivach 1999; Tuplin 1999.55–57. For early references to foreign languages, see e.g. Anacreon fr. 423 Page; Hipponax' frr. 3a, 92 West. Farina 1963.25–29. The word *barbaros* connotes intellectual inferiority already in Heraclitus DK I⁶, 22, B107.

[10] Long 1984.130–131; E. Hall 1989.3–5. For *barbarophōnos* applied to the Persians in a derogatory context, see the oracles in Herodotus 8.20.2 and 9.43.3 ('barbarian-voiced scream': βαρβαρόφωνον ἰυγήν).

[11] See especially Bacon 1961.15–24, 64–73, 115–120, who usefully surveys all references to foreign speaking in the three tragedians.

bewildering sounds of a strange language.[12] In the *Suppliants* the Danaids refer to their own foreign way of speaking, and the Egyptian herald provides a demonstration of un-Greek phrasing.[13] Fifth-century comedy imitates barbarian gibberish or barbarized Greek.[14] Several passages in various texts compare barbarian speech to the voice of animals, especially birds.[15] Pindar associates the adjective *barbaros* with *palinglōssos* 'with the tongue put on backwards' (*Isthmian* 2.24), and Sophocles' *Trachinian Women* replaces the antithesis "Greek and barbarian" with "Greek and *aglōssos*," 'tongueless' (1060).

If language comes to represent a mark of Greekness and Greek superiority,[16] and if the issue of cultural differentiation is central to the *Histories*, what views does this text communicate about Greek as a language and the various barbarian languages?[17] Does the role Herodotus attributes to language reinforce or undermine the authoritative Greek-barbarian antithesis of contemporary thought? The *Histories* resound with many different discourses in the voices of the narrator-historian, the narrator-ethnographer, characters, ethnographic subjects, and sources. Everyone speaks Greek, but the text provides irregular indications that in the world of the story they did not. Narratives of past events mention linguistic discrepancies among the speakers or give us glimpses of a community's speaking style. Ethnographic descriptions include the language of this or that people along with other cultural

[12] Broadhead 1960.xxx; Bacon 1961.23; E. Hall 1989.76–79; Colvin 1999.77–78, 85. Aeschylus *Persians* 20–58, 302–330, 402, 958–972, 981–984, 994–1001; at 634, βάρβαρα σαφηνῆ ἱέντος 'speaking in clear barbarian language' (uttered by a Persian) comes across as ironic.

[13] Bacon 1961.15; *Suppl.* 117–119, 127–129, 825–902, 914, 972–974. Cf. Aeschylus *Agamemnon* 1059–1061; 1062–1063, esp. 1050–1053 (ἀγνῶτα φωνήν of Cassandra); Sophocles *Trachinian Women* 1060; *Antigone* 1001–1002; *Ajax* 1262–1263; Euripides *Orestes* 1369 ff.; fr. 139 N²; *Phoenician Women* 1302–1303, *Bacchae* 158–159; *Rhesus* 294–297. Aristophanes *Birds* 199–200; *Frogs* 679–682; *Women at the Thesmophoria* 1082–1135, 1176–1226.

[14] Long 1984; E. Hall 1989.17–21; Colvin 1999.287–295. See especially the speech of the Persian "Eye of the King" in *Acharnians* 100 and of the Triballian god in *Birds* 1615, 1628–1629 discussed with references by Long 1984.134–135 and Colvin 1999.288–290. Elsewhere in comedy (e.g. the Scythian archer in *Women at the Thesmophoria* 1678–1679) the barbarian speaks bad Greek, as does the Persian prisoner in Timotheus' nome *Persians* (158–173). Colvin 1999.55–56. See below, p. 70 and note 10.

[15] E.g. Aeschylus *Agamemnon* 1050 (barbarian speech of Cassandra like the voice of swallows); *Seven Against Thebes* 463–464 (horses blowing a barbarian noise); Sophocles *Antigone* 1001 (birds with barbarian cry); Aristophanes *Birds* 199–200; Schol. *Birds* 1680 (Triballian god sounds like swallow); *Frogs* 679–683 (swallow on lips of Cleophon). For a later example, see the language of the satyr in Plutarch *Sulla* 27.2. Other passages in Harrison 1998, note 80; Moggi 1991.38–39.

[16] E. Hall 1989.4. *Contra* J. Hall 1995.93–95.

[17] For recent discussions of foreign languages in Herodotus, see Harrison 1999; Chamberlain 1999; Campos Daroca 1992; Colvin 1999.57–61.

traits. The narrator discusses the reality of language difference for a traveler in distant lands and shows what non-standard speech sounds like when he explains foreign names or introduces native terms.

These different passages do not create a monolithic representation of the importance of language differentiation; they are sometimes hard to interpret, mutually contradictory, answering or even neutralizing one another. The linguistic discrepancies recorded in the text are part of a broader cultural and ideological heteroglossia at different levels of discourse.[18] We can separate the voice of the *histōr* from the speeches and traditions he reports, but only up to a point.[19] The primary narrator sometimes appears to slide along the ideological spectrum in response to his sources, material and audiences. On the whole, however, the *Histories* display a view of language that is internally coherent and consistent with Herodotus' message on other aspects of culture.

Within the ideological landscape of the Greek-barbarian antithesis, Herodotus paradoxically distinguishes himself for being both uniquely *philobarbaros* and uniquely Greek.[20] He appears uniquely Greek in the sense that even among fifth-century Greek texts his work professes an extraordinary degree of commitment to freedom and democratic equality. The *Histories* thereby celebrate the superiority of a culture that at a certain point in its development chose to implement various forms of broad-based constitutional government.[21] But Herodotus is also *philobarbaros*. His political egalitarianism is grafted onto the Ionian tradition of objective description of foreign peoples and shares in the broad-minded outlook of the sophists and it therefore extends horizontally beyond the boundaries of the Greek world.[22] In his mythical reconstruction of the origin of civil society, Plato's Protagoras attributes

---

[18] For Bakhtin's term heteroglossia see note 3, above.

[19] Dewald 1987, esp. 153, was the first to call *histōr* the narrator and implied author who emerges from the *Histories* as opposed to the real author (on these distinctions, see Booth 1983.67–77; Chatman 1978.147–158; Genette 1980.213–214). Though never used by Herodotus, the term is especially apt and now accepted by many modern critics. Besides referring to the practice of *historiē*, it carries a juridical meaning that is also appropriate to Herodotus' authorial persona and activity. See especially Nagy 1990.262, 315–320; also Connor 1993.

[20] For Herodotus *philobarbaros*, see Plutarch *Malice of Herodotus* 12–14 = *Moralia* 857A–F.

[21] See especially 5.78. Loraux 1986.205. The notion of Greek equality is sometimes expressed in terms of the Greeks' adoption of a constitutional order and rejection of autocratic rule; e.g. Hippocrates *Airs, Waters, Places* 23; Aristotle *Politics* 1237b.23–34. For the origins and character of Greek ideas of freedom and equality and their limitations from a modern viewpoint, see Morris 1996, Ostwald 1996, Hansen 1996, Raaflaub 1996, Roberts 1966.

[22] See, e.g 2.3.2; 3.38. For the objective aspect of early Greek ethnography, see Fornara 1983.12; Nippel 2002.278, 282–287. For Herodotus' link with the sophistic and scientific thought of his time, see Thomas 2000.

the "civic art" not to Athenians or Greeks but rather to "all men."[23] Similarly in Herodotus, just as the citizens of the Greek *polis* share in political decisions, and the various *poleis* are, or deserve to be, autonomous, so also "all men" are competent to pursue knowledge and regulate themselves.[24] Or, to reverse this principle in the direction of the ethnographer's work, a study of the *nomoi* ('customs') of different societies will display in most cases the equal competence of all men. This view appears almost closer to our modern American pluralistic ideology than to the most commonplace attitude of fifth-century Greeks. One of the central tasks of Herodotus' work is in fact to promote the paradox that the uniqueness of Greek values also entails respect for the equal worth of non-Greeks.[25]

The overarching thesis of this book is that the issue of language provides Herodotus with special opportunities to instruct his audiences. In Chapter One we begin by examining Herodotus' attitude to the Greek linguistic community, his notions about the boundaries that separate it from non-Greeks, and his view of its internal differentiation both diachronically (different origins of the different groups of Greeks) and synchronically (different dialects). Chapter Two will turn to the ways in which the ethnographer Herodotus deals with languages not his own as a special trait of the foreign cultures he describes and as a factor to be reckoned with in the course of "field work." Perhaps our most precious passages from the point of view of Herodotus' ideology of language are the passages where Herodotus asserts his authority as interpreter by translating foreign words: these "metanarrative glosses," scattered through both ethnographic descriptions and historical sections in the *Histories*, are the special focus of Chapter Three.[26] Finally, in Chapter Four, we shall examine the role of language difference in several narratives that explicitly mention the issue as an element of the plot. The preponderance of all this evidence in the *Histories* confirms Herodotus' commitment to the notion of the equal competence of foreign societies in various spheres. It also shows that language

[23] Plato *Protagoras* 320c–323c. Roberts 1996.188. Herodotus (in a passage possibly derived from Protagoras) insists on Persian awareness of the nature of different forms of government, including democracy (3.80–83; 6), while at the same time noticing the imperfect fulfillment of the principles of freedom and democratic equality among the Greeks. On the connection between Herodotus and Protagoras, see Thomas 2000.125–127, 147–149, Munson 2001.165–166, 206–207.

[24] Herodotus is also explicit in assuming the equality (ἴσον) of all men in the sphere of religious beliefs at 2.3.1.

[25] 3.38. Munson 2001.168–172.

[26] According to my definition, a gloss is a metanarrative statement in the voice of the narrator explaining some element of the text. See Munson 2001.32–44 for different types.

difference is not a serious obstacle to understanding others, enhances rather than hampers learning about foreign cultures, and helps people to understand their own culture. Different aspects or mediums of communication provide abundant opportunities for uncertainty and error.[27] But language in the strictest sense is to Herodotus an area of objective and interesting difference (and unexpected similarities) that also turns out to be relatively unproblematic. It therefore represents a good model for coming to terms with other more emotionally charged features of the barbarian world.

[27] Though Herodotus is an expert interpreter of all types of codes of information. See especially Hollmann 1998 and Hollmann, forthcoming. I am grateful to the author for providing me with a typescript of the latter work.

1

GREEK SPEAKERS

Greeks and Pelasgians

IN HIS NARRATIVE OF MILTIADES' CONQUEST OF LEMNOS (6.137–140), Herodotus begins by reporting how at that time Pelasgians were occupying the island. In the heroic age these Pelasgians used to live in Attica but the Athenians expelled them, "either justly or unjustly," depending on the source one believes. According to Hecataeus, the Athenians had allowed the Pelasgians to inhabit an infertile piece of Attica below Hymettus in exchange for their building the wall around the Acropolis; but when the Pelasgians transformed the land by cultivating it, the Athenians became envious and drove them out. The Athenians themselves, by contrast, claim that they expelled the Pelasgians because they had violated the Athenian women and planned an attack against Athens (6.137). These are the two versions of the story, concludes the narrator, and he declines to choose between them.[1]

From Attica the Pelasgians went to Lemnos, where they sought revenge from the Athenians for depriving them of their previous home. They raided Brauron during the festival and abducted a number of Athenian women whom they kept as concubines. The children born from these unions learned from their mothers "the Attic language and Athenian customs" (γλῶσσάν τε τὴν Ἀττικὴν καὶ τρόπους τοὺς Ἀθηναίους), formed a tight group among themselves, and soon "felt entitled to rule the other children and were much stronger" (ἄρχειν τε τῶν παίδων ἐδικαίευν καὶ πολλῷ ἐπεκράτευν. Cf. ἄρχειν πειρῷατο, 6.138.3). This worried the Pelasgian men, who then slaughtered the children together with their Attic mothers (6.138). Here the narrator explains that this crime and an earlier symmetrical female one—when the Lemnian women murdered their husbands—have become proverbial, so that "people throughout Greece term all atrocious deeds 'Lemnian'" (6.138.4). The

---

[1] For their origin, see Bertelli 2001.87–88. I follow the edition of the *Histories* by Hude.

murderous Pelasgians were subsequently struck by a curse and received a Delphic prescription that they pay the requisite penalty to the Athenians. Many years later this came to pass when they were forced to turn their island over to Miltiades (6.139–140).

Hecataeus' version of the Pelagians' expulsion from Attica presents them as master builders and farmers—a "culture-hero-type people"; in the Athenian version they are lawless barbarians.[2] The Lemnian section of the narrative, though it lacks a visible source, confirms Athenian moral claims.[3] Athenian fifth-century imperialism finds its justification in the brutal behavior of the heroic-age Pelasgians and their inferiority to the Athenians on the basis of ethnicity and culture, including language.[4]

Athenians, Pelasgians, their mutual relations and their respective languages are treated somewhat differently in an explanatory passage where the narrator discusses the ethnic origins of the Greek people. In lieu of the contrast we have just seen between Athenians and Pelasgians (corresponding to the Greek-barbarian antithesis), here Herodotus emphasizes the descent of the Athenians from the Pelasgians by connecting it to an original ethnic divide within the Greek world between Spartans and Athenians. The *genos* ('descent group') of the Spartans is Doric, he says, that of the Athenians Ionic. The Spartans were Greeks who, after a great deal of wandering, settled in the Peloponnese.[5] The Athenians, by contrast, were in ancient times a Pelasgian *ethnos* ('nation', in the broader sense) and never left their homeland (1.56.2–3).[6]

After connecting the Athenians with the Pelasgians, the narrator proceeds to identify the latter as non-Greek with a cautious argument that reveals the subtext of an opposing tradition.[7] Precisely what language the

---

[2] Sourvinou-Inwood 2003.136.

[3] Cf. 4.145.2. The Athenian claim to moral superiority at 6.137.4 in turn recalls claims to superior justice in the exercise of power that we find in fifth-century Athenian diplomatic discourse; see Thucydides 1.75.1–4.

[4] The reference to the story of the ethnic dominance of the children of the Attic women in Lemnos seems to allude to Pericles' citizen law of 451 BC, which prescribed Athenian descent also from the mother's side. Cartledge 1993.21, 26; Dewald 1998.692. On Pericles' citizenship law, see esp. Cartledge 1993.73.

[5] See J. Hall 1987.62, 1997.41–51; 2002: 25–29, 82. Malkin 1994.41–42.

[6] On the terms *ethnos* and *genos*, see Walbank 2002.24; Jones 1996; J. Hall 1997.35–36. Barbarians/ Pelasgians are the original inhabitants of Hellas also at 2.52–56 (Hellas as a whole), 1.146.1, 2.171, 7.94, (Arcadia/Peloponnese), 2.51.2, 7.94 (Attica); 2.52 (Dodona), 7.42, 95 (Aeolis).

[7] On the wide spectrum of views concerning the barbarian or Greek ethnicity of the Pelasgians in ancient authors after Homer, see Sourvinou-Inwood 2003.117–121.

ancient Pelasgians spoke is impossible to know, he says, but the evidence of those Pelasgians presently living in Thrace and the Hellespont indicates that "the Pelasgians were speakers of a barbarian language."[8] The Attic Pelasgians adopted a new language when they became Greek (1.57.2–3), in contrast with the original Greeks (i.e., the Dorians), who always spoke the same language, that is to say, Greek (1.58.1).[9]

This disquisition on origins is not irreconcilable with the story in book 6 about the Athenians expelling the Pelasgians from Attica and Lemnos.[10] But it speaks in a different style (argumentative rather than narrative) and uses a different code (scientific rather than moral or political).[11] At the same time, it also creates a polemic in the text by emphasizing the notion of a barbarian origin of the Athenians. The Lemnian passage, as we have seen, reproduces Athenian hegemonic propaganda about the Athenians' superior Greekness. The discussion on origins reshapes and corrects this sort of discourse.

Herodotus' Pelasgian theory goes along with contemporary self-representation of the Athenians as autochthonous to the land they currently inhabit and opposite in this respect to the Spartans.[12] Herodotus, however, declines to follow the Athenian myth in one respect: its insistence on equating "autochthonous" to Greece (or "Pelasgian") with proto-Greek and therefore, so to speak, "super-Greek."[13] Similarly, as he confirms the Spartan national myth of origin, Herodotus stops short of mentioning the role of the native

---

[8] This is Herodotus' original contribution to the "Pelasgian theory" of the ancients, (Myres 1907.197–203) and one of the few investigations in Herodotus that are linguistic in the proper sense of the word (Campos Daroca 1992.49).

[9] I agree with the interpretation of 1.58 by Sourvinou-Inwood 2003.122–124, but the passage is ambiguous. Cf. McNeal 1985.17–20; Lévy 1991.220.

[10] See especially Sourvinou-Inwood 2003. At the factual level, see Myres 1907.192, 201. Myres (who is attempting to extract from ancient sources historical information on the Pelasgians) regards the Pelasgians "who settled below Hymettus" of Herodotus 6.137.2 as a wave of (Hellespontine) Pelasgians that came later, when the Pelasgians of Attica had already been Hellenized. This is to some extent supported by 2.51, which talks about "Pelasgians who became neighbors of the Athenians in Attica when these were already counted as Greeks," except that the same passage says that also these Pelasgians eventually began to be regarded as Greeks. See Laird 1933.

[11] McNeal 1985, Georges 1994.131–133, 137; Thomas 2000.119–122, 216; 2001.222–223.

[12] Cf. Herodotus 7.161.3, 9; Thucydides 1.2.1–3.4, 4.109.4. On Athenian historical and mythical discourse on autochthony, see Loraux 1993, esp. 37–71; Rosivach 1987; Connor 1993a.204–206; Georges 1994.135–136; Isaac 2004.114–124.

[13] Cf. Plato, *Menexenus* 245c–d; Lysias 2.17–18; Loraux 1993.50–51; Rosivach 1987.302–303; Georges 1994.135; Dougherty 1996; Hall 1997.54; 2002.142; Thomas 2001.218. In Aeschylus *Suppliants* the Pelasgians of Argos clearly count as Greeks and symbolically represent the Athenians. Georges 1994.164, E. Hall 2002.142–143.

Heraclids, whose leadership of the Dorians increased the legitimacy of their invasion of the Peloponnese.[14] Herodotus' distribution of credentials in the pedigrees of Attic and Dorian Greeks responds to the contemporary competition for full Greekness by recontextualizing Solon's maxim that one cannot have everything (1.32.8). It is either Hellenic from the start and adventitious to Greece, or indigenous and with barbarian roots.[15]

Pelasgians and barbarians

The Pelasgians murder the Attic-speaking children (6.138) because they perceive them as being a threatening ethnic elite. In the closely parallel case of the Scythian king Scyles, on the other hand, the king's bilingualism is the first step in a cultural shift that represents, from the Scythian viewpoint, not the acquisition of an unfair advantage but a descent into barbarism.[16] The introduction of a bilingual minority in a culture may either contribute to violence or achieve brilliant results.[17] On a more global scale, however, Herodotus' discussion of origins envisions a change of language as "the sign and instrument" of the cultural integration of barbarians crossing over to Greekness in the course of time.[18] The Hellenization is represented as beneficial to all the parties involved: the present day *Hellēnikon ethnos*, ethnically mixed, has grown more numerous and stronger than those residual Pelasgians who never learned Greek or the original core of Dorian Greek-speakers (1.58).

As they become Greek by learning Greek, barbarians enrich Greek culture, including the linguistic field.[19] Because the Pelasgians in Herodotus represent

---

[14] Cf. 6.52.1, 9.26.2–4, 27 and the genealogies of the Spartan kings at 7.204, 8.131.2; cf. 5.72. Malkin 1994.33–43; J. Hall 1997.56–65.

[15] The usual antonyms are *autokthōn* (αὐτόχθων) and *epēlus* (ἔπηλυς), though Herodotus uses neither term in this passage (but see 1.171–172, 176.3, 4.197.2). Rosivach 1987.297–299. That *barbaroi* inhabited the Peloponnese before the arrival of the Greeks is already found in Hecataeus *FGrHist* 1 F 119 (= Strabo 7.7.1, C321).

[16] 4.78–79, esp. 78.1; Campos Daroca 1992.45; Munson 2001.118–123. Cf. Harrison 1998, ch. 2, "Herodotus' knowledge of foreign languages."

[17] Compare the slaughter of the Median boys by Cyaxares' Scythian guests (1.73) with Psammetichus' successful "Greek language program" (2.154; see below, p. 28–29).

[18] The quoted expression is from Campos Daroca 1992.46; see also McNeal 1985; Asheri 1988.299; J. Hall 2002.194. That other factors were involved in the transition is implied by the wording ἅμα τῇ μεταβολῇ τῇ ἐς Ἕλληνας καὶ τὴν γλῶσσαν μετέμαθε (1.57.3).

[19] Notably by the importation of the alphabet, which Herodotus attributes to the Phoenician companions of Cadmus (5.58).

the collective embodiment of what links the Greeks to the non-Greek world, they are especially responsible for fundamental contributions at the intersection of language and religion. In another innovative passage, Herodotus declares that the Pelasgians learned from the Egyptians the "names" (*ounomata*) of most of the gods, devised a few of them themselves, and transmitted them to the Greeks.[20] This means, at the very least, that the Pelasgians learned to distinguish different divine figures by their functions and attributes and then gave each of these figures a name.[21] Herodotus, however, does not make clear in what linguistic form the Greeks received the Egyptian divine names via the Pelasgian intermediaries.[22] Were these the names the Egyptians still currently use, although their Greek counterparts now differ from them? Herodotus himself elsewhere says that the Egyptians call Apollo *Horus*, *Osiris* is Dionysus in Greek, and so on.[23] If the Pelasgians received these Egyptian names, did the Greeks eventually change or "translate" them into Greek? This could have happened as part of the codification effected by Homer and Hesiod, which included, Herodotus says, adopting new divine "names" (*epōnumias*).[24] Or are the current Egyptian names Herodotus records perhaps alternative or

---

[20] 2.50.1–3 (cf. 2.4.2): from Egypt came all the gods except for the Dioscouri, Hera, Hestia, Themis, the Graces, and the Nereids, who are of Pelasgian origin, and Poseidon, who comes from Libya. For the polemical style of this discussion, see Thomas 2000.282.

[21] 2.53. Linforth 1926; 1940; and see especially Burkert 1985 (cf. 1970.445–446), followed by Campos Daroca 1992.108. Thomas 2000.275–278. Mikalson 2003.167–173.

[22] Hence the scholarly controversy centered on the meaning of the term *ounoma* as Herodotus uses it, especially in this passage—whether it must necessarily denote the very word composed of determinate sounds or letters, or whether it can more generally refer to the conceptual representation that name expresses, in whatever language. See the summary of the controversy in Lloyd 1976.203–205 and, most recently, the discussion by Harrison 2000.251–264. Irad Malkin explains in the following linguistic terms of the open–ended polytheistic mentality of the Greeks and other ancient peoples: "The gods of 'others' were either unfamiliar ('new gods') or, simply the 'same', but known by different names and attributes. Religion was *langue*; the names of their gods and their particular cults were *parole*. For example, when Herodotus says that 'Ammon is the name of Zeus among the Egyptians' (2.42), he sees a 'Zeus' in the Egyptian deity (*langue*), although his name, cult and even status may be peculiarly Egyptian (*parole*). In other words, he was saying, 'Ammon is how you say 'Zeus' in Egyptian'" (Malkin 2004.350). In the terms of this passage, it appears that the word οὐνόματα at 2.50.1–3 has shifted semantically from the realm of *parole* to that of *langue*.

[23] 2.156.5; 144.3. For Herodotus' translations of the names of several foreign divinities, including Egyptian, see p. 31 and note 5.

[24] 2.53.2. Epōnumia (ἐπωνυμία) can be used as a synonym of *ounoma* (οὔνομα; compare, for example 2.4.2 with 2.52.2), though it is generally interpreted as "epithet" in this passage (see e.g. Lloyd 1976.250). The difference is more properly that *epōnumia* tends to refer to a motivated name (given for some reason or after something or somebody, as at 4.45.2, where both terms occur). Campos Daroca 1992.85. For the term *onoma* (ὄνομα), see also below, p. 31–32.

later forms, while the originals that spread to Greece resembled the names by which the Greeks called their gods in Herodotus' time?[25]

Herodotus' lack of specificity on the form of the names at 2.50 reveals that for him the most concrete linguistic dimension of the barbarian religious contribution the Pelasgians transmitted to Greek culture is here of secondary importance.[26] By the same token, this section also confuses the issue of what language the Pelasgians themselves spoke at the time they adopted divine names. Herodotus says that before learning (mostly from the Egyptians) about individual figures of gods, the Pelasgians conceived of them as a collectivity and called them *theoi* because divine beings "put things in order" (κόσμῳ θέντες, 2.52.1). Now, this is a competent word, one that testifies to a degree of philosophical speculation about the nature of things.[27] Moreover it looks like Greek, and its form and etymology point to resemblances between a barbarian language and Greek.[28] Alternatively, if this is supposed to represent a genuine Greek word, it indicates that the Pelasgians' native tongue was at this point Greek, even though Herodotus still calls them "Pelasgians."[29] In the discussion on ethnic origins, as we have already seen, Herodotus is deliberate in identifying the Pelasgians as original speakers of a *barbaros glōssa*

---

[25] Lattimore 1939; Lloyd 1976.204; Harrison 1998.4 "The Imagined Relationship between Greek and Foreign Languages"; 2000.256.

[26] 1.131.2 suggests that Herodotus' translations of the names of the gods might be more conceptual than linguistic: "The Persians call the whole vault of the sky 'Zeus'." On the other hand at 4.59.1–2 (see below, p. 44), the translation of the concept is accompanied by an etymological translation.

[27] See also the later Pelasgian name of the goddess Themis (2.50). Cf. Aristotle's idea of god as holding things together (*On the Cosmos* 397b10–401b24; *Politics* 1326a32). The etymology also recalls those of the Derveni commentator and of Plato's *Cratylus*. See below, p. 22, note 18; p. 36.

[28] For foreign words transparent to Greek in Herodotus, see Chamberlain 1999, who greatly emphasizes Herodotus' sensitivity to "the occasional transparency of one language from the point of view of another (especially from the Greek point of view), and the role played in that transparency by minimal phonic changes" (Chamberlain 1999.278). Obviously transparent foreign terms in Herodotus include the Scythian *Papaios* for Zeus at 4.59.2; *Porata*/Pyretos at 4.48.2; the Persian kings' names at 6.98.3; *Masistius*/Makistius at 9.25.1; and the possibly "Egyptian" *barbaroi* at 2.158.5. See below, pp. 35, 44, 48–50, 65. Plutarch's tendency in *On Isis and Osiris* to translate Egyptian names through the Greek is noticed by Donadoni 1947.

[29] See also the ancient Greek-speakers of Dodona at 2.54–57, at a time when "Greece was called Pelasgia" (2.56.2). On the apparent lack of clarity in Herodotus' treatment of the Pelasgians (which Myres 1907 and Laird 1933 attempt to dispel), see e.g. Campos Daroca 1992.75; Georges 1994.133–134; Thomas 2001.226–227; Sourvinou-Inwood 2003.121–131. For *ethnea* that are linguistically on the margin between the Greek and the barbarian world in historical times, see the Geloni, an originally Greek population of Scythia who speak a mixed Greek-Scythian language (4.108.2); and the Eretrians deported to Ardericca of Cissia, who "kept their old language" (6.119.4). The blurring of the boundaries is partially due to the unpredictable movement of peoples in the course of history (5.9.3).

'barbarian language' (1.57.3) who ceased to be Pelasgian and became Greek once they learned Greek. Here, by exploiting the instability of the tradition about the ethnic identity of the Pelasgians, he makes them into a benevolent *tertium quid* that has bridged the gap between the Greek and the barbarian world.[30] In ancient Dodona, the center where cross-cultural trends join, the Pelasgians are equally at home in the antitheses "Pelasgians and Barbarians" and "Pelasgians and Greeks":

> When the *Pelasgians* asked at Dodona if they could adopt the names of the gods that came from *barbarians*, the oracle bid them to use them ... The *Greeks* later inherited these names from the *Pelasgians*.
>
> 2.52.3

In the *Histories*, in other words, the Pelasgians are archetypal hybrids, in turn barbarian-speaking and Greek- (or Greek-like-) speaking, lawless primitives, immaculate agriculturists of the Attic soil, religious teachers of the Greeks, perpetrators of crimes "all the Greeks call Lemnian," and autochthonous ancestors of the Athenians. They are contradictory because they embody Herodotus' fluid notion of ethnic mixture and his resistance to crystallize contemporary constructs or gloss over their illogical aspects. For him ethnicity is something hard to pin down since, among other things, it fluctuates between language and languages, between distinction and affinity on the basis of speech.[31]

Greek language and languages

If pre-history sometimes blurs the distinction between Greek and barbarian-speakers, in Herodotus' time the Greek world is linguistically differentiated from within according to ethnic, regional, or political lines. The abstract notion of a single Greek "language," taken for granted in the discussion of the Hellenization of the Pelasgians and many other passages, coexists with the reality of different Hellenic dialects, also termed, in most cases, *glōssai* or *phōnai*.[32] In the Lemnian narrative, the "language" in question is not Greek

---

[30] See Sourvinou-Inwood 2003, esp. 121–131.

[31] On the confusion of linguistic boundaries in Euripides, see S. Saïd 2002.69, 89.

[32] Mosley 1971.1–2; Morpurgo Davis 2002.157, 169. J. Hall 1995.93; 1997.168–177; Harrison 1998; Colvin 1999.33–38. On Greek dialect difference, see esp. Thucydides 3.94.5, 4.3.3, 41.2, 112.4, 7.44.6, 57; Plato *Cratylus* 385d–e, 401c etc. (Rochette 1996.95–96); Xenophon *Anabasis* 3.1.26; and Aeschylus *Seven Against Thebes*, where an all-Greek *heterophōnos stratos* (ἐτερόφωνος στρατός) comes complete with barbarously whistling horses (170, 463). See S. Saïd 2002.89; Colvin 1999.75.

but Attic: *hē Attikē glōssa*.[33] Not only does Herodotus mention Ionian/Dorian variations (1.139), he also emphasizes in surprisingly strong terms that the Ionians "do not speak the same language" but four completely different ones (1.142.3–4).[34] This area of "disagreement" (ὁμολογέουσι . . . οὐδέν) coexists with other unrelated internal differences, such as the Ionians' heterogeneous ethnic origin and the political disunity that causes their repeated subjection to foreign powers.[35]

In the *Histories*, the narrator explains of how certain words are used in different parts of Greece; these notices outnumber those marking terms and expressions shared throughout Greece, like "Lemnian deeds."[36] Glosses to local Greek codes often testify to the peculiarity of local institutions or the cultural foreignness of certain areas of Greece.[37] Evidence of this sort not only puts into question the uniformity of "the Greeks" at the linguistic and cultural levels, it also detracts from the main separation between the Greek and the barbarian worlds.[38]

---

[33] 6.138.2. Cf. Solon fr. 36.8–12, on Athenians sold abroad who no longer speak Attic. Athenian belief in the superiority of the Attic dialect seems to have increased in the fourth and third centuries (Isocrates *Antidosis* 295–296; Posidippus fr. 28 Kock). Colvin 1999.28–29. On the other hand, in the fifth century, the "Old Oligarch" complains that the Attic dialect is uniquely contaminated by barbarian speech ("Xenophon" 2.7–8).

[34] On 1.139 (Dorian *san*/Ionian *sigma*), see below, p. 26. J. Hall 1997.152; 1985.86–89. For quotations of poetry and oracles in the epic-Ionic dialect, see Colvin 1999.60. For the Greek consciousness of internal language differentiation at the local level in the fifth century, see Hainsworth 1967.66–67.

[35] Cf. 1.146. Asheri 1988.348. Campos Daroca 1992.42 observes that the linguistic differentiation noted by Herodotus (unverifiable for us on the basis of the epigraphic evidence) is part of his polemic against the Ionians; thus the Samians, who deserted at Lade, form a linguistic group by themselves.

[36] 6.138.4 (see above, p. 7). See also 1.193.5 ("the palm trees *which the Greeks call 'male'*"); 3.111.2 (cinnamon); 4.14.3 (poem *Arimaspea*), 4.189.2 (name of *aigis* of Athena). Some passages, where the name-users are implicitly Greek, rather refer to people in general: 4.45.2–5 ("Europe," "Asia," "Libya"), 3.33 ("sacred disease"), 3.122.2 ("the so-called 'human generation'," as opposed to the heroic age of Greek tradition). For Greek expressions for barbarian realities, see below, p. 33 and note 17.

[37] The following are Spartan terms: 1.67.5, ἀγαθοεργοί; 6.57.2, Πύθιοι; 6.71.1, Zeuxidamos; 7.134, Talthybiads; 8.124.3, ἱππεῖς; for 9.11.2, see below, p. 16. For words from other parts of Greece, see 1.14.3, Γυγάδας; 4.18.1, Βορυσθενεῖται/'Ολβιοπολῖται; 5.58, Φοινικήια and διφθέραι; 5.77.2, ἱπποβόται; 7.176.3, Χύτροι; 7.188.2, Ἑλλησποντίης; 7.197.2, λήιτον; 8.52.1, Ἀρήιος πάγος. A difference in terminology between Athenians and Boeotians on a borderline pass is noted at 9.39.1, Τρεῖς κεφαλαί/Δρυὸς κεφαλαί.

[38] Cf. Plato *Protagoras* 341c, which labels Lesbian Greek as a *barbaros phōnē*.

Barbarians and strangers

In his description of the antithetical origins of Spartans and Athenians in Book 1, Herodotus shows the roots of a profound split in the Greek world at the time of his narration.[39] His stay-at-home proto-Athenians and wandering proto-Spartans ironically reverse the polar stereotypes applied to their descendants on the eve of the Peloponnesian war.[40] Towards the end of the *Histories*, however, we find a statement of unity that transcends these division: "*to Hellēnikon* ('the Hellenic nation', or perhaps, 'the Hellenic thing', or more simply 'the Greeks') means having the same blood, same language, common sanctuaries of the gods and sacrifices, and similar customs" (τὸ Ἑλληνικόν, ἐὸν ὅμαιμον καὶ ὁμόγλωσσον, καὶ θεῶν ἱδρύματά τε κοινὰ καὶ θυσίαι ἤθεά τε ὁμότροπα, 8.144.2). Here the Athenians, who are the speakers, extend the criteria of their Attic identity in the Lemnian passage (γλῶσσα and τρόποι, 6.138.3) beyond the confines of the city-state.[41]

In the face of the Persian threat, the passage just cited represents a plausible oppositional definition of what it means to be Greek.[42] It does not matter so much that in the rest of the *Histories* the issue of blood is treated with a certain irony and that cultural factors are not always reliable criteria of Greek ethnicity.[43] What affects the status of this passage is rather the narrative context: it fails to verify the definition of Greekness and reproduces instead, once again, the dialogism between an authoritative "nationalist" Greek ideology and a more skeptical view.[44] Elsewhere in the *Histories*, the Persian general Mardonius says that the Greeks, since they are *homoglōssoi* ('speakers

[39] Asheri 1988.297.

[40] 1.56.2. Contrast the portrayal of fifth-century Athenians and Spartans in Thucydides 1.70–71.

[41] On the double aspect of Greek identity expressed in this speech, see Moggi 1991.32.

[42] As J. Hall (1995.92–93) observes, "the sometimes heterogeneous behavior of Greeks could begin to appear more uniform by contrast with the more alien practices of others."

[43] Thomas 2001. On similarities between different cultures in Herodotus, see Pelling 1997, Munson 2001.91–132. For "common blood" as an ethnic construct, cf. the rhetoric of Aristagoras at 5.49 with the narrator's statements at 1.146–147 (mixed blood of the Ionians) and 1.151.2 (Methymnans of Lesbos enslave inhabitants of Arisba in spite of their common blood ties). Beside the Pelasgian origin of the Ionians, Herodotus also records the foreign origin of Greek aristocratic families (5.57, 5.66, two passages which Plutarch *Malice of Herodotus* 26 = *Moralia* 860E, regards as insulting; 6.53–54, on the Heraclids of Sparta; cf. 2.91), and the Greek ancestry of foreign peoples or dynasties (1.7). Lévy 1991.220–221.

[44] Gould (1989.5) assumes that the Athenian definition represents a direct expression of Herodotus' thought; J. Hall (1995.92; 1997.44–45; 2002.189–194) even argues that it constitutes a Herodotean innovation rather than a commonplace among fifth-century Greeks. But see Fornara 1972.84–86; also Raaflaub 1987.240; Georges 1994.130–131; Thomas 2001.214–215.

of the same language'), should stop fighting and rather settle disputes by heralds and messengers (7.9.β2). Here, on the eve of an invasion by the same Mardonius, embassies come and go and a quarrel arises among the Greeks. Their political disunity devalues the ethnic and cultural homogeneity to which they lay claim.[45] The idea of a unified Greek nation will symbolically run aground, at the end of the scene, on a minor issue of language.

The narrative sequence begins with the arrival at Athens of Alexander of Macedon, a figure who straddles the boundary between the Greek and barbarian worlds: a man officially declared Greek and an official friend (*proxenos*) of Athens, he is also related by marriage to the Persian king.[46] As a messenger of Mardonius, he now brings to the Athenians the offer of a separate peace with Xerxes. The Spartans are worried by this overture because oracles predict that an alliance of Persians and Athenians will one day expel them from the Peloponnese. They send messengers to Athens and argue that it would not be right for the Athenians to listen to Alexander and come to terms with the enemy. The one is a tyrant and friend of tyrants, they say; the others are *barbaroi* and cannot be trusted by Greeks (8.142.1–5).

The Athenians refuse to negotiate with the Persians, but they need help for the resistance and repeatedly urge the reluctant Spartans to send it. In their first speech they proclaim they will never make peace with the invader for two reasons: they need to avenge the harm he has done to their *polis*, and they remain loyal to the common heritage of the Hellenes—defined in the passage quoted above (8.144). In a second speech, they complain that by their delay the Spartans are betraying the Greeks and recall how advantageous the terms of the Persian peace would be for themselves (9.6; 7α.1–2). Finally, in the face of further Spartan stonewalling, the Athenians intimate in a third speech that they are ready to become the allies of the King and follow him wherever he might lead (9.11.1–2).

This crescendo of Athenian appeals, protests, and threats never meets with an articulate response. But the Spartans, in the meantime, realize what danger they are in and take action in secret. At the last minute they inform the exasperated Athenians that their army is already on its way to central Greece, marching, as they say, "against the foreigners" (ἐπὶ τοὺς ξείνους, 9.11.2). Here Herodotus translates: "*Foreigners* (ξείνους) is what they called the barbarians" (9.11.3).

[45] Campos Daroca 1992.48. Cf. Finley 1975.120–123.

[46] Herodotus 8.136–139; cf. 5.21–22; 7.173.3; 8.34. In the case of the Macedonian royal family, by "Greek" Herodotus means Achaean (5.22). Badian 1994.

16

The narrator's intervention guarantees that we do not miss the Spartan linguistic marker and the information it conveys:[47] at a time between the massacre of their own at Thermopylae and another battle with the Persians, the Spartans do not acknowledge the distinction between *barbaroi* and *xenoi* ('foreigners'). This seals the implicit response of the text to the initial Greek-barbarian opposition and the Athenians' definition of Greekness on the basis of, among other things, language.[48] Fifth-century Greeks normally called *xenoi* Greeks from other city-states or individual non-Greeks with whom they could envision relations of guest-friendship.[49] The term may underline the outsider position of certain Greeks with respect to others, but it shortens the distance between barbarians and Greeks. Herodotus' Spartans, who call other Greeks *xenoi* more frequently than anyone else, are also the only Greeks who apply the word to non-Greeks.[50] They consider all non-Spartans as foreigners, to be feared (or not) in about the same way (8.141.1).

In more general terms, the linguistic variant used by the Spartans confirms certain contradictions that Herodotus elsewhere attributes to them. Most Hellenic of the Hellenes, they are culturally closest to the non-Greek

---

[47] For markers, see Colvin 1999.21–26. In this case Colvin rightly notices, however (1999.59), that if the tradition is correct the Spartan lexical choice appears in its Ionic form (*xeinous* [ξείνους] as opposed to *xenous* [ξένους]). This is consistent with Herodotus' practice when he reports speeches of non-Ionians.

[48] *Pace* Jones 1996.315n4. From the point of view of the historical context of 479 BC, of course, the Spartan choice of words, if genuine, may be taken as reflecting the less polarized attitude of the Greeks in general before the Persian Wars (above, p. 2 and note 9); so Malkin 2004.349. Herodotus, at any rate, implies that it was almost inconceivable in his time.

[49] Cartledge 1993.47. Cf. Moggi 1992.34: from the Greek point of view, the foreignness of the *xenos* is political, that of barbarians is also ethnic and cultural. Of course, barbarians of different *ethnea* (except for the Egyptians: see below, p. 65) refer to the Greeks, and each other, as *xenoi*.

[50] The Spartan Amompharetus applies the word again to the Persians at 9.53.2. Contrast, in addition to the Spartan ambassadors' references to "barbarians" at 8.142.1 and 5 (cited above, p. 16), Pausanias' distinction at 9.79.1. When all the characters involved are Greek, the vocative *xeine* (ξεῖνε), is either uttered by a Spartan or addressed to a Spartan for a total of nine times out of ten (uttered by a Spartan: 5.49.9, 50.3, 9.79.1, 91.1 and 2, plus the inscription at 7.228.6; addressed to a Spartan: 1.68.2, 5.72.3, 7.160.1; single exception: 7.162.2). In other grammatical cases *xeinos* and *xeinoi* appear in the mouth of a Spartan (3.148.2, 5.51.2, 6.86b1, 7.226.2) or are used to denote strangers from the Spartan point of view (1.65.1, 3.55.2, 9.9.1, 9.91.1) or in reference to a Spartan (6.81) for a total of nine times out of eleven. (I have not counted instances where *xeinos* is used with the dative in the sense of 'guest-friend of': see Powell 1938, ad loc.) According to Herodotus' account, lack of contacts with foreigners had been one of the problems in pre-Lycurgan Sparta (1.65.2), but for other sources this was still the case in the fifth century. Among the various stereotypes applied to the Spartans in Attic comedy (on which see Harvey 1994 esp. 39), we find the epithet *dieironoxenoi*, 'treacherous toward outsiders' in Aristophanes *Peace* 623.

world.[51] They are the original speakers of Greek, yet peculiar and primitive in matters of speech.[52] In the sequence we have considered, Spartan reticence and Athenian eloquence symbolize a broader cultural gap between these two groups of Greeks, namely their political incompatibility and inability to communicate. Herodotus' narrative, in this case, validates unskilled Spartan speech to the detriment of Athenian rhetoric. The notion of *to Hellēnikon* appears as a noble ideal, but its uncertain historical relevance undermines the distinction between *barbaroi* and *xenoi*.

---

[51] On Spartan foreignness, see e.g. 6.58–60. Hartog 1988.152–156; Cartledge 1993.81; Munson 1993; 2001.96.

[52] Cf. Thucydides 4.40.2. Colvin (1999.70–73, esp. 70) observes that when Xenophon "add[s] dialect colouring to a reported speech, it is always the Laconian dialect that is in question." On Spartan local terms in Herodotus, see above, note 37; for Laconian brevity, see 3.46, 9.90–91, 7.226.1–2 and cf. Sthenelaidas in Thucydides 1.86.1. For silence in Spartan life, see David 1999.

2

THE ETHNOGRAPHER AND FOREIGN LANGUAGES

Another *histōr*: Psammetichus and the origin of language

O NE PASSAGE IN THE *HISTORIES* appears to raise the anthropological problem of the beginning of human speech and therefore, potentially, of the origin of language differentiation. But it does so in an indirect way, through the eyes of the Egyptian king Psammetichus who is, moreover, interested in a different problem. Psammetichus "wants to know" what nation in the world is the oldest, since the Egyptians have always claimed that they were. With both the power and the inclination to undertake a controlled experiment, Psammetichus isolates two infants from all cultural contacts to see what language (φωνήν, 2.2.3) they will speak after they stop making meaningless noises.[1] He places the children in a remote hut, where only a shepherd is to go in and feed them milk every day by bringing his goats to them, but without ever talking to them or speaking in their presence. After about two years, the children greet the shepherd by clasping his knees, stretching their hands to him, and uttering their first word, *bekós*,[2] which turns out to be Phrygian for 'bread'. Faced with the recurrence of this behavior, Psammetichus acknowledges that the Phrygians are the oldest people of mankind and the Egyptians must be second.[3] This, at any rate, is the Egyptian story. At its conclusion Herodotus mentions, and rejects as a typical idiocy, a Greek variant according to which Psammetichus entrusted

---

[1] On kings-*histōres* in Herodotus, see Christ 1994. On the relative infrequency of controlled experiments in Greek science, see G. E. R. Lloyd 1966.73–79.

[2] Actually called an *epos* (ἔπος), or "'word' broadly and in the sense of *parole*, that is an utterance which here happens to be in the form of one word. What the children are . . . saying is 'Give us bread!'" (Hollmann 2000.221).

[3] 2.2.1–5. On this passage, see Salmon 1956; Benardete 1969.32–33; Lloyd 1976.5; Campos Daroca 1992.50–55; Christ 1994.84–86; Vannicelli 1998; Dewald 1998.615.

the children not to a shepherd with goats but to women whose tongues had been chopped off.[4]

From the point of view of the text the focus of this sequence is clearly not the origin of language, but rather the very process of scientific and historical inquiry and its limitations.[5] Among the various inquirers, narrators, and data-interpreters who participate in the narrative, Psammetichus takes all possible care to reproduce artificially the conditions of primitive man for the purposes of his inquiry; he is humane and responsible, as well as ready to accept the politically unwelcome results.[6] The Egyptians in general agree with his conclusions; they preserve the correct memory of the event. The Egyptian priests tell the story to Herodotus, who in turn uses it as a sort of proem to the report of his own investigations on Egypt. The Greeks, irrelevant in every other way, only appear as negative models to show how one people can distort another people's traditions.[7]

But if Psammetichus is a benign figure and a model for Herodotus himself, he also unwittingly demonstrates (and Herodotus, through him, demonstrates to his audience) that researchers, no matter how resourceful and well intentioned, will not be able to answer all questions nor will they always be aware of the unexamined assumptions that may lead them to believe they can.[8] The most remarkable feature of the Psammetichus sequence is in fact Herodotus' failure to corroborate the king's interpretation of his experiment. Its results, as far as the text is concerned, remain ambiguous.[9]

Psammetichus emerges as relatively open-minded with regard to the question he expects the experiment to answer: "What is the oldest people of mankind?" (even though his assigning second place to the Egyptians appears arbitrary). That he tries to find this out through language, however, reveals he has already made up his mind with respect to the underlying issue, the origin of human speech. Psammetichus would not proceed as he does if he did not assume at the outset that innate to all men is not merely the potential for

---

[4] 2.2.5. Most scholars believe that the first story is also of Greek origin (see Vannicelli 1997.203), but Herodotus clearly distinguishes an Egyptian and a Greek version.

[5] Dewald 1998.615.

[6] Christ 1994.186.

[7] Cf. 2.45. Munson 2001a.141–142.

[8] At 2.28.4, Herodotus also criticizes the experiment by which Psammetichus attempted to discover the depth of the springs of the Nile, thereby trying again, in the words of Vannicelli 1998.204, "to test the limits (spatial, this time) of human knowledge." Christ 1994.171–172.

[9] Griffiths 2001.164. Later Herodotus even appears to disregard Psammetichus' findings: 2.15.2–3 (on the antiquity of the Egyptians); 7.73 (on the Phrygians; but see Vannicelli 1997.207–209).

speech and communication, but also a specific primordial language (which he then recognizes to be Phrygian), with ready-made original words signifying what most men have in common, such as bread.[10] Alternative views on the origin of language were certainly available in Herodotus' time, but it is hard to assess whether more of his listeners would have marveled at the ingenuity of the experiment or laughed at Psammetichus' interpretation of its results. Several texts describe linguistic expression as predominantly a matter of culture. In Plato's version of Protagoras' myth about the origin of mankind, for example, speech develops over time as a social accomplishment (*Protagoras* 322a). The author of the *Dissoi Logoi*, a fourth-century tract perhaps inspired again by Protagoras, mentions the fact that a Greek infant raised in Persia will learn Persian and a Persian infant raised in Greece will learn Greek; this proves that we learn our words, we are not born knowing them.[11] Democritus seems to have described a situation in which different groupings of primitive men, internally interacting with one another, devise different languages.[12] In conjunction with the treatment of language elsewhere in the *Histories*, these fifth-century insights suggest that Herodotus is sharing with his audience the ironical awareness that Psammetichus' experiment has a meaning different from that which the king attributes to it.[13]

The children have never had experience of Phrygian, and no word from it or from any other existing "language" (*phōnē* in the sense of *glōssa*) would spontaneously come to them. *Bekós* is a plausible sound for both human infants and animals, and ancient readers already explained it as the children's imitation of the only *phōnē* (or 'voice') they have heard, the bleating of the goats.[14] This derivation would not make *bekós* a random sound (see ἀσήμων

---

[10] Human beings are bread-eaters by definition in Homer: see e.g. *Iliad* 13.321–322, *Odyssey* 9.191, Vernant 1989, and Detienne 1977 passim, esp. 117. Vannicelli 1997.205–207. Herodotus' long-lived Ethiopians are an exception (3.22.4).

[11] DK 90 B 6.12. Robinson 1979.51–59.

[12] Diodorus Siculus 1.8.3–4 (cf. Vitr. 33.24–28), on whose derivation from Democritus, see Cole 1990.60–69. Guthrie 1965.474–475; Rochette 1996.10. On Democritus' conventional theory of language, see also Classen 1976.242–245. Contrast Epicurus *Letter to Herodotus* (DL 10. 75), where language difference depends on the different natures (*phuseis*) of *ethnea* inhabiting different places. Donadoni 1986.194 quotes a passage of the Egyptian *Hymn to Aten* in which the god himself has provided for the needs of different peoples of the world, also assigning to each its own language.

[13] Benardete 1969.33; Campos Daroca, 1992.50–55; *contra* Salmon 1956.329.

[14] Scholium on Apollonius Rhodius *Argonautica* IV 257, 62c; scholium of Tzetzes on Aristophanes *Clouds* 398a; Suidas s.v. βεκεσέληνε. The Greek version Herodotus rejects, where goats are

κνυζημάτων at 2.2.3), in the same way as the children's clasping of the knees and the stretching of the hands are clearly not random movements. Though it cannot mean 'bread', which the children have never seen and cannot name, *bekós* might still express an instinctive need (e.g. solid food, after all that milk), and as soon as the children utter it, it becomes a "word."[15] But while some gestures may be assigned, as in this case, to an apparently innate and universal code, all words reproduce other available sounds or words; they will therefore develop differently depending on the environment of the speakers.[16]

If these considerations indicate that the text wants us to interpret Psammetichus' experiment from a conventionalist point of view, the Egyptian king's belief in ready-made natural words is not unthinkable either, by fifth-century standards.[17] Plato's *Cratylus* features a debate about whether language is related to the world by nature or by convention; conceivably, the former view can lead to the theory of a "natural" (that is to say, cosmic or divine) origin of *onomata* ('names' or 'words'). This concept does not explicitly appear in the *Cratylus*, but the pre-Socratic commentator of the Orphic *Theogony* upholds it in the Derveni Papyrus.[18] In the story of Psammetichus' experiment, moreover, since the non-verbal act of supplication of the children, which we would regard as highly conventional, is certainly not learned from the goats but innate, the same could be said for their first word.[19]

If we follow Psammetichus' and the Egyptians' "natural" interpretation, the discovery of the original human language does not help to explain why all nations do not call bread *bekós* in the same way as they all suppli-

---

replaced by mute women, would eliminate this level of meaning. Dover 1993.219 cites βρύ ('drink') as a baby word in connection to the βρεκεκεκέξ sound of Aristophanic frogs. For the difference and overlap between *glõtta* and *phõnē*, see below, note 24.

[15] See above, note 2.

[16] For stretching of the hands in sign of entreaty or supplication, cf., e.g.1.45.1 (Adrastus, coincidentally a Phrygian); 4.136.1 (Persian soldiers); 7.233.1 (Thebans). Clasping of knees: 1.112.1 (Median woman); 9.76 (Greek woman). Lateiner 1987.113. For other apparently cross-cultural gestures, see 4.113.2 (below, pp. 72–73).

[17] Scholars of the old school have been reluctant to accept this, heaping contempt on the naïveté of either Psammetichus and the Egyptians (here mocked by Herodotus, according to Benardete 1969.33) or Herodotus himself (Salmon 1956.329: "Nous ne croyons pas qu'on ait jamais presenté Hérodote comme une des grandes intelligences de l'antiquité").

[18] The Derveni Papyrus was provisionally published by Merkelbach 1982.1–12; see also Laks and Most 1997; Burkert 1970; 1985.128–129; Baxter 1992.130–139. For the suggestion that names derive from a superhuman power, see also *Cratylus* 438c (cf. 397c). Guthrie 1965.474, 1969.204–219. For the connection between the Derveni papyrus and the *Cratylus*, see Kahn 1997.

[19] On the distinction between ritualized or conventional and other types of gestures in Herodotus, see Lateiner 1987, esp. 90–92 and his chart on pp. 113–116. See also above, note 16.

cate by extending their hands.[20] If, conversely, Psammetichus' experiment ironically confirms that humans grow up learning speech from what they hear, it provides no information on who the first human speakers were nor what words they spoke. But the issues of first speech or speakers are clearly secondary in the *Histories*. Herodotus does not debate the Egyptian priests on the anthropological meaning of Psammetichus' experiment, somewhat as, in the proem to the whole work, he declines to respond to the mythical explanations of the Persian *logioi* ('experts of traditions in prose').[21] In history Herodotus can only productively inquire into events not too distant in time. In ethnography he focuses on current realities, such as the existence of many languages. Languages are, like other *nomoi*, mysterious in their origin but observable and synchronically comparable by one who studies differences and affinities among men in all areas of culture.

Languages and cultures

In Herodotus' ethnographic descriptions, language both unifies and divides *ethnea* ('peoples') around the world in not entirely predictable ways. The distinction is no longer simply, as in the Pelasgian passage, between Greek and an unspecified "barbarian language" (1.57.2), but among Scythian, Persian, Egyptian and so on, as well as many "special languages" of smaller nations. In his relentless pursuit for what is the same and what is not, Herodotus records, for example, linguistic differentiation within a single large *ethnos* or geographical area.[22] Thus at the Eastern extremities of the earth, the Indians include "many peoples (ἔθνεα), who do not speak the same language (οὐκ ὁμόφωνα σφίσι); some are nomadic and some not" (3.98.3). In the Scythian North, not everyone speaks Scythian and distinguishing among different languages helps to prevent inaccurate generalizations.[23] The cannibalistic *Androphagoi*, who are obviously unique in all respects (ἴδιον ἔθνος, 4.18.3), also

---

[20] Campos Daroca observes that the Psammetichus episode is the reverse of the tower of Babel story because it illustrates the origin of language, but not that of different languages (1992.52).

[21] 1.1–5. For analogies between the two passages, see Campos Daroca 1992.5, who draws attention to *logioi* at 1.1 and *logiōtatoi* at 2.3.1 and 77.1. See also the parallel between what Herodotus himself "knows" (οἶδα) at 1.5.3 and what he "thinks" (δοκέω) at 2.15.3. Vannicelli 1997.212–216. According to Dewald 1998.615, each passage represents "a thematic introduction to a research-driven narrative." For *logioi* as 'experts of traditions in prose' see Nagy 1988.181–182 and 1990.223–224.

[22] Campos Daroca 1992.40–42.

[23] Campos Daroca 1992.41. See Munson 2001.79–82.

have a language of their own (γλῶσσαν ... ἰδίην, 4.106); so do the Bald People or *Argippaei*, sharply identified by their peculiar somatic characteristics, diet, and customs as well as language (φωνήν ... ἰδίην, 4.23.2).[24]

Language is only one of the criteria that determine ethnic identity, and it does so to a varying degree.[25] A peoples' language, usually in addition to other traits, may be different from that of their neighbors and similar to that of their distant nation of origin. The Colchians, for example, descend from the ancient Egyptians left behind by Sesostris' army and they are similar to the Egyptians in language and their way of life (2.105).[26] Budini and Geloni, whom the Greeks confuse, "do not speak the same language and their material culture is not the same" (4.109.1). The Geloni are originally Greek, live in a *polis* of wood, honor Greek gods, eat grain, and speak a language (γλώσση) that is partly Scythian and partly Greek (4.108.2). In a poignant case, Hellenicity wins over territorial dislocation of a violent sort: the Eretrians whom Darius has deported to Ardericca of Cissia still preserve, to Herodotus' day, their ancestral language.[27]

Other times the narrative distinguishes one people from another only by language and one other trait, but not by other characteristics. The Eastern Ethiopians in Xerxes' army, for example, were only different from the Western Ethiopians "in language and hair" (7.70.1). Conversely, the Sagartians, who are both ethnically and linguistically Persian, wore equipment with mixed Persian and Pactyan features (7.85). In the case of the Carians and Caunians, language appears to count for little as a criterion of identity. The Caunians have a language that has become very similar to that of the Carians (or perhaps the other way around), but they are very different from them and, indeed, from the rest of mankind in customs and religion (1.172.1). The Carians, for their part, consider themselves related to Lydians and Mysians, whose eponymous ances-

---

[24] Most of these statements, formulated in terms of "same" and "not same," constitute in fact glosses of comparison. For the role of comparison in Herodotus' descriptions of foreign peoples, see Munson 2001.91–100. As these two passages show, *glōssa* and *phōnē* can be synonymous. However, the latter may also indicate inarticulate sounds or the voice of animals. Long 1987.114; Campos Daroca 1992. Accordingly, Herodotus uses either term for obscure, marginal, or unknown languages (including at 2.2.3, considered above, pp. 19 and 21), but tends not to apply *phōnē* to mainstream languages such as Persian, Egyptian or Greek. At 2.55.2 and 2.57.2, we find a merely apparent exception, when Herodotus' Pelasgian sources call an unintelligible language, which they do not realize is Egyptian, a "*phōnē* of birds" in contrast to the "human *phōnē*" of intelligible Greek. See below, pp. 67–69.

[25] Lejeune 1940–1948.54; Lévy 1991.219.

[26] See also 1.57.3 (Crestonians and inhabitants of Plakia); 2.42.4 (Ammonians); 4.117 (Sauromatae).

[27] 6.119.4. On dislocation and nostalgia in Herodotus, see Friedman 2004.

tors were the brothers of their own. Consequently, the Carians admit Lydians and Mysians to their temple of Zeus in Mylasa, but exclude those who are not from their same *ethnos* even though they speak the same language (1.171.5–6). Descent and religion, rather than language, are here the unifying factors.[28]

In these contexts, Herodotus has almost no other way of characterizing a *glōssa* or *phōnē* linguistically, except to say that it is similar or different with respect to the language of someone else.[29] The flatness of these references also prevents them from suggesting any evaluation of the different languages themselves, even though speech or other aspects of certain cultures may point to a varying degree of primitivity. Differing in language and *diaitē* ('way of life') from the *quasi*-Greek speaking Geloni, the Budini are nomadic and eat lice (4.109.1). A unique attempt at a more colorful description leads Herodotus into the derogatory stereotype that other Greek texts apply to all kinds of barbarian speech.[30] The Ethiopian troglodytes, who eat snakes and lizards and are hunting quarry for the neighboring Garamantes "have a language that is like no other, for they squeak like bats."[31] When faced with the truly unfamiliar sound of a people's language, even modern ethnographers find it hard to avoid this type of parallel.[32]

As uninformative as they are, Herodotus' recurring reminders of a people's different or special speech confirms that language constitutes a branch of the ethnographer's study of *nomoi, diaita,* and *ēthea*.[33] On a few occasions he attempts to establish a more substantive connection between a linguistic phenomenon and specific features of a culture. The etymology of the word *theoi* 'gods', which the Pelasgians invented to denote the gods collectively, is linguistic evidence for this ancient people's religious beliefs.[34] The matrilineal system that makes the Lycians unique has an idiomatic aspect: the Lycians take their names from their mothers, not their fathers

---

[28] Campos Daroca 1992.41.

[29] See also the four "entirely different" Ionian dialects (1.142.3; above, p. 14). Lejeune 1940–1948.55; Campos Daroca 1992.42, 56.

[30] See above, p. 3 and note 15.

[31] 4.183.4. For Libya as a land of linguistic anomalies, see Campos Daroca 1992.58, 74. A more prosaic evaluation which correlates primitive language and primitive culture is in Thucydides' description of the Aetolian tribe of the Eurytanians: ἀγνωστότατοι . . . γλῶσσαν καὶ ὠμόφαγοι 'speaking a most unintelligible language and eaters of raw meat' (Thucydides 3.94.5).

[32] So Bailey 1983.53, on the language of the Dowayos: "a crude, unsubtle instrument, little better than animal cries . . . ."

[33] Diels 1910.82; Cardona 1970.20–24.

[34] 2.52.1. See above, p. 12.

(1.173.4–5).[35] Certain wretched tribesmen in the heart of Libya, who use curses and foul words against the scorching sun, bear the collective name of Atarantes, but do not have individual names (4.184.2–3). For the Persians, conversely, personal names are an important reflection of their self-image and culture. The narrator suggests this point deliberately, framing it with introductory and concluding statements that refer to the process of *historiē*:

> And also this other thing happens to occur among them (συμπέπτωκε), which has escaped the notice of the Persians them-selves but not us: Their names, which are equal (ὅμοια) to their bodies or magnificence, all end with the same letter, the one the Dorians call *san* and the Ionians *sigma*. If you pay close attention, you will find that Persian names end in this letter, not just some of them and not others, but all in the same way (ὁμοίως).
>
> 1.139

From the point of view of their meaning, Persian names connote magnificence (μεγαλοπρεπείη), which coincides with the Persian penchant for external display in the preceding sections of Herodotus' ethnography.[36] From the point of view of morphology, the consistency of the linguistic rule—"not some of them and not others, but all in the same way"—fits in with the overall "regularity" that characterizes Persian social norms.[37]

In this passage, Persian unity contrasts with the fragmentation of the Greeks, who even use two different names for a single letter, the Dorian *san* and the Ionian *sigma*.[38] But in the Ionian ethnography, which as we have seen thematizes Ionian disunity in language and other respects,[39] Herodotus remarks that the Ionians, and the Greeks in general, have names for their festi-

---

[35] Campos Daroca 1992.41.

[36] Esp. 1.133–36. Cf. the names at 6.98 (below, p. 48).

[37] For the interpretation of this passage I here essentially follow the path of Wolff 1934.161 and Immerwahr 1966.186n111. Persian culture is one that admits of no exceptions; see e.g. 1.137.2. *Contra* Harrison 1998, ch. 3 "The Greek conceptualization of foreign languages." For a more philosophical view on 1.139, see Chamberlain 1999.292–296. His interpretation is bold, but has the merit of taking maximum notice of Herodotus' idea of the relation between an object and its name and of the importance Herodotus gives to the forms of names; it also explains the extraordinary emphasis in this passage on the narrator's superior awareness and his address to the listener. On the basis for Herodotus' statement on the ending of Persian names, see below, p. 27.

[38] Linguistic and idiomatic variations within the Greek-speaking world recorded by Herodotus are listed above, p. 14 and note 37.

[39] See above, p. 14.

vals that "all end with the same letter [*alpha* in this case], *just as Persians names do*" (1.148.2). This gloss formulates an opposition, rather than an analogy, between a unified linguistic rule and the disunity of the society to which the rule belongs. Just as 1.139 looks forward to the Ionian passage by mentioning in implicit antithesis to the Persian rule the *san/sigma* split among the Greeks, so 1.148.2 explicitly looks back precisely to 1.139 by drawing a limited analogy between Ionians and Persians in the linguistic sphere. The way in which the two passages cross-reference each other and provide complementary indices of analogy and opposition is evidence of Herodotus' unresolved reflection of the possible relationships between languages and cultures.

Foreign languages and *historiē*

It is hard to believe that Herodotus maintains that all Persian names end in "s" only because he is deceived by the Greek transcription of masculine Persian names.[40] His characteristically elliptical style seems to have obscured his reference to a phenomenon we are no longer in a position to appreciate very well. This may be, in fact, one of the few passages in the *Histories* that look at a foreign language from the viewpoints of both speaking/hearing and writing/reading. Herodotus' observation that the final "s" "escapes the Persians themselves" may point to the fact that he knew, no less than modern scholars, that no *letter* (*gramma*) corresponding to *san/sigma* appeared at the end of Persian names in their written form. But he also appears to have known that the Persians pronounced the *sound*, which one would expect them to acknowledge with a sign.[41]

The phenomenon of the vanishing "s" in Persian names leads the narrator to imply that he and perhaps other outsiders like him (ἡμέας) are more attuned to noticing certain linguistic peculiarities than the native speakers, and he invites the listener to join him in the process of observation (ἐς τοῦτο διζήμενος εὑρήσεις).[42] Of the possible disadvantages of being an outsider we hear nothing.[43] Herodotus' glosses of *historiē* elsewhere in the

---

[40] This is a commonly held opinion (see especially Meyer 1862.194; Diels 1910.85), but then what about Scythian, Egyptian, and other names? I am indebted to Michael Flower for helping me come to terms with this passage. For Medo-Persian names in Herodotus, see Schmitt 1976, Armayor 1978.

[41] See Legrand 1946.155; cf. Evans 1991.139n203.

[42] It is not clear whether "we" here means "I," "we the Greeks," or some other group. For the difficulties in interpreting the first person plural in Herodotus, see Chamberlain 2001.

[43] For the problems of language comprehension that the real author Herodotus would have encoun-

work rather insist that the undeniable reality of language differentiation does not in the least hamper inquiry about foreign peoples. Because speech is in any case translatable, there are linguistic interpreters (*hermēneis*), whose job is apparently far easier than that of religious or mantic interpreters.[44] In the historical narrative, these bilingual professionals are instruments of the kings' power over multiethnic empires.[45] But in the ethnographic sections and in the narrator's accounts of his own research, they appear to be easily available to ordinary travelers. The polyphonic northeastern region of Europe, for example, is entirely accessible (περιφάνεια), at least as far as speakers can be found.[46] "Because," says the *histōr*, "there are Scythians who get to these populations and it is not difficult to learn things from them . . . . The Scythians who come to them transact their business through seven interpreters and seven languages."[47] In Egypt, the same king Psammetichus who performed the linguistic experiment we have seen sent some Egyptian children to learn Greek from the Ionians, the first *alloglōssoi* ('speakers of a different language') who came to reside in his land (2.154.1–5). Establishing a hereditary cast of

tered in his study of foreign cultures, see the vivid description by Gould 1989.24–27. Gehman 1914.9–12 collects remarks by ancient authors on difficulties caused by a difference of language.

[44] This is the meaning of the word before Herodotus (who reserves it for linguistic interpreters), aside from Aeschylus *Agamemnon* 1062–1063 (but cf. 616). Lejeune 1940–1948.58; Rotolo 1972.396–397. Campos Daroca 1992.63. For professional interpreters of oracles, omens, and dreams in Herodotus (*khrēsmologoi, manteis, oneiropoloi*), see Hollmann 1998.221–226 and Hollmann, forthcoming. In Plato's *Cratylus* (407e–408a) a *hermēneus* (ἑρμηνεύς) is an interpreter of speech (*logos* [λόγος]), if not specifically of foreign languages. For interpreters of foreign languages in Greek and Roman sources, see Gehman 1914, esp.16–53.

[45] Campos Daroca 1992.63–68. See below, pp. 73–77.

[46] Only beyond the Bald Men the *eremos*, a physical barrier empty of men, breaks the chain of communications, thereby precluding inquiry (4.25). See Romm 1992.36–37. Cobet 1971.94.

[47] 4.24. Of the ethnic groups living above Olbia surveyed at 4.18–23, the number of those speaking Scythian or a mixed Scythian language can in fact be reckoned at seven (Scythians, Sauromatians, Budini, Geloni, Thyssagetae, Iyrcae, Argippaeans, according to Rawlinson 1880.1.21, and cf. Corcella 1993.253). One is tempted, however, to regard the number as symbolic (Fehling 1989.100), as in the *heptaglōssos* lyre of Pindar *Nemean* 5.24, seven-stringed and therefore able to perform a variety of local melodic patterns or *nomoi* (Nagy 1990.90, 355). Cf. also the North Carolina expression "to be silent in seven languages," quoted by Safire 1999. These metaphors signify that a clear message can be conveyed through several different linguistic codes, used individually or in combination.

interpreters may have been one of Psammetichus' ways of segregating the foreigners, but for Herodotus it opened up Egypt to the Greeks.[48] One of these Egyptian interpreters once assisted Herodotus himself by deciphering for him an inscription on the base of the Great Pyramid of Cheops.[49] Many other times in the Egyptian *logos* the *histōr* reports his interviews with the Egyptian priests or other local sources, and no intermediary enters the picture.[50]

The unproblematic way in which the narrator deals with foreign languages has nothing to do with the actual linguistic competence of the real author Herodotus. Experts in the field rate this rather low by our standards since they regard it as consistent with the obstinate monolingualism of the ancient Greeks in general, at least in the mainland.[51] What is important for an ideological assessment of the text is rather that the *histōr* Herodotus—the narrator who emerges from the work itself—is, in his own way, a multilingual character, familiar with the principal languages, at ease with languages, and interested in the world's heteroglossia in the linguistic, as in the cultural, sphere.

---

[48] Donadoni 1986.204–205.

[49] 2.125.6. A unique case, as Hartog 1988.239 remarks. West 1985 discusses this and the other inscriptions cited by Herodotus (about half of them foreign).

[50] For the frequency of these glosses in Book 2, see Marincola 1987. At 2.105, Herodotus reports to have spoken with both Egyptians and Colchians.

[51] E.g. Meyer 1862.192–195; Legrand 1932.74–76. See especially the discussion and bibliography in Harrison 1998, ch. 1 ("Herodotus' knowledge of foreign languages"). The suggestion by Mandell 1990 that Herodotus must have known Aramaic is not convincing. On Greek monolingualism and lack of interest in foreign languages see especially Momigliano 1975a and 1975b esp. 15. Also Lejeune 1940–1948.57; Rotolo 1972.395–396; Hartog 1988.38–39; Campos Daroca 1992.27; Colvin 1999.70. See however the "Old Oligarch's" complaint that, unlike the other Greeks, the Athenians use a mixture of culture traits, including language, from all Greeks and barbarians ("Xenophon" *Constitution of the Athenians* 2.8).

3

HERODOTOS HERMĒNEUS

Metalinguistic glosses

ERODOTUS HIMSELF ASSUMES THE ROLE OF INTERPRETER when he translates a foreign word into Greek or provides a native term. Aside from Psammetichus' discovery that *bekós* is Phrygian for bread (2.2), all switches of the linguistic code in the *Histories* occur in metanarrative.[1] In about twenty cases the narrator deliberately introduces a common noun denoting some object found in a foreign land (e.g. "a plant they call so and so").[2] When the linguistic switch proceeds in the other direction, Herodotus' linguistic glosses occasionally serve to translate foreign common nouns that appear in the narrative or in the utterance of a character, according to a pattern familiar in modern fiction.[3] For the most part, however, they give some explanation for proper names of individuals, peoples, or places either by translating the word etymologically into Greek or by mentioning an alternative name in Greek (what "the Greeks call x").[4] Translations of proper names also include passages

---

[1] Campos Daroca 1992.76. These translations have been discussed by Hartog 1988.237–248 ("Translating, Naming, Classifying"); Harrison 1998 (with complete lists); Chamberlain 1999.

[2] See below, p. 53 and note 106. Marked introductions of proper names are of course usually not as significant. A historical work is bound to mention foreign names of persons and places and the marked form for introducing these (e.g. 2.156.1: "an island *called* Chemmis"; 155.2: "*the name of this city is Buto*") is extremely common and merely constitutes a metanarrative mediation by which the narrator acknowledges the audience's lack of familiarity with the subject. See, however, 2.164.2, 4.18, 7.64, 89.2 for more notable cases. In some important instances a barbarian proper name is given only to be translated back etymologically into Greek (2.30.1, 4.27, 4.52.3, 4.110.1), and those will be discussed below, pp. 36–38.

[3] 2.143.4; see also 2.158.5 (below, p. 64). More approximately: 4.7.3 with 4.31; 4.27.4; 4.155.2–3 (below, pp. 35, 82). Cf. Prince 1977.2–3 for modern examples.

[4] For translation in the strict sense vs. explanation or the giving of an alternative name, see Chamberlain 1999. These glosses are about twenty-five. I am not here counting eponymic derivations of ethnic names (e.g., "The Persians derive their *epōnumiē* from Perse," 7.61.3), also frequent

that place the foreign name of a divinity side by side with the Greek. Here the pattern tends to proceed from the familiar Greek name: "In Egyptian, Apollo is _Horus_, Demeter _Isis_, and Artemis _Boubastis_."[5] Another type of translation is represented by six glosses that explain what a measurement by foreign standards "means" (_dunatai_) when converted into Greek standards.[6]

Unless Herodotus is explaining a local Greek term, most translations involve the actual appearance of barbarian names, terms, or loan words in the text.[7] Some glosses, however, state that a foreign people call _x_ by a certain word, and the word given is Greek, perhaps implicitly representing the translation of a local foreign term which the narrator does not give.[8]

Though the categories I have mentioned more or less coincide with the modern distinction between proper names and common nouns, such distinction should not be pressed too far. In the fifth century, _onoma_ is the only Greek term that denotes a single word as a grammatical and phonetic entity,[9] as opposed to an utterance (_epos_, _logos_, _rhēma_, or _rhēsis_), which occasionally

---

in the logographers (e.g. Hecataeus, _FGrHist_ 1 F 266, 307, 308). These often occur in conjunction with glosses that record the ancient name or a name-change of a people or place; see 1.171, 173.2, 3, 7.170.2, the numerous instances found in the catalogue of Xerxes' force (e.g. 7.61.2), and the notation on the name of the Ammonians at 2.42.5. Müller 1972.113. Campos Daroca 1992.92–95.

[5] 2.156.5. See also 1.199.3 ("the Assyrians call Aphrodite _Melitta_"); 2.42.5 ("the Egyptians call Zeus _Amon_"); 2.46.4 ("in Egyptian this goat and Pan are called _Mendes_"; 2.79.3 ("in Egyptian Linus is called _Maneros_"); 4.59.2 ("in Scythian, Hestia is called _Tabiti_, Zeus . . . _Papaios_, Earth _Api_, Apollo _Goetosyrus_, Heavenly Aphrodite _Argimpasa_, Poseidon _Thagimasadas_") The foreign name appears first at 2.144.3 ("_Osiris_ is Dionysus in the Greek language"). At 4.180.2 ("the indigenous goddess whom we call Athena") the Libyan name is not given; see also 2.122.1 ("he went down to what the Greeks believe to be Hades"). Linforth 1926. Lattimore 1939.

[6] 1.192.3; 2.6.3; 2.168.1; 3.89.2; 5.52.6–53; 6.42.2. Chamberlain 1999.275–276.

[7] For Greek into Greek translations, see above, p. 14 and note 37.

[8] 2.171.1 ("a ritual that the Egyptians call _mysteria_"); 3.31.2 ("Royal Judges"); 3.79.3 (_magophonia_); 4.31 ("feathers"), 4.181.4 ("Spring of the Sun"), and perhaps, though in some of these cases the namers may be Greek, 2.36.3 ("emmer"); 2. 62.1 ("Lamplight festival"); 2.72 (fish called "lepidotos"); 2.112.2 (sanctuary of "Foreign Aphrodite"); 2.148.1 ("City of the Crocodiles"); 2.164.2 (_Makhimoi_); 4.107 (_Melankhlainai_); 4.52.1 ("Mother of Hypanis"; see below, p. 44); 4.192.3 (species of Libyan mice given in Greek), 7.188.3 ("Ovens" of Mount Pelion). Especially interesting in this category are the glosses at 3.93.2=7.80 (_anaspastoi_: see Asheri 1988b.158) and 7.83.1, cf. 7.211.1 (_athanatoi_: see Pagliaro 1954.146–151). See also, possibly, 1. 132.3 ("theogony"), 2.158.5 ("barbarians"). The possibility that 4.20.1, τὰ καλεύμενα βασιλήια, may be rendering a native term in Greek translation is discussed by Kothe 1969.75–79. How and Wells 1928.ii.303, following Stein interpret the reference to the blind slaves of the Scythians (4.2, 4.20.1) as Herodotus' misunderstanding of the etymology of the Scythian word for "slave"; the narrator, however, does not present the word _tuphlos_ (τυφλός) as a translation.

[9] Other than the related _epōnumia_. See above, p. 11 and note 24.

may consist of a single word.[10] Both proper and common names (as well as participles and adjectives) are included in the Greek category of *onomata*, and language is viewed as a collection of "names" for things that exist in the world.[11] Herodotus does not discuss terms denoting virtues or other abstract concepts that some of his contemporaries analyzed in Greek.[12] He gives *cultural* translations of what Persians, Scythians and so on call (for example) "courage" by mentioning the types of behaviors that would be labeled as "courageous" in those foreign cultural codes.[13] But the range of his linguistic translations is more limited: names of individual human beings and gods, of ethnic and other groups, of institutions, customs, places, geographical features, animals, plants, and items of material culture. Herodotus' interest in language, at any rate, has mainly to do with the participation in the *Histories* of peoples from different cultures; it is related to the narrator's broader project of explaining them to his own audience.

Hartog rightly observed that from an ethnographic viewpoint these interventions tend to have a contradictory effect. On the one hand, translation is a bridge that gives a means of access to a distant environment. On the other hand, the translation or, even more, the deliberate introduction of a foreign word, emphasizes the gap between "here" and "over there."[14] It remains now to be seen how specific cases produce these effects. Herodotus' linguistic glosses are both something more and something different than rhetorical displays of exoticism and professional competence, as Hartog seems to maintain. Through them the narrator assigns to himself and to his audience specific ideological positions with regard to the speech of the *barbaroi*.

---

[10] On these terms, see Hollmann 2000, who shows that in two cases in Herodotus the term *epos* is used in reference to a single word, but both times it actually denotes an utterance that implies a whole proposition. The first case is "*bekós*"in the story of Psammetichus' experiment (called an *epos* at 2.2.4); see above pp. 19–23). The second is *Asmach* at 2.30.1 (for which see below, pp. 37–38). Hollmann 2000.220–221. In the fourth century, the term *rhēma* began to denote a "verb" as opposed to a "noun" (*onoma*). We find this distinction, for example, in Plato's *Cratylus* 425a, although elsewhere in the same dialogue (399b) *rhēma* is a "phrase" in contrast to *onoma*, a single word. See LSJ *ad voces*. See also Aristotle's definitions (*Poetics* 1457a; *On Interpretation* 16a–b) distinguishing names from verbs (Kraus 1987.45). For *rhēsis*, see esp. below, p. 40.

[11] Guthrie 1969.204–219. Burkert 1985.127. Hartog 1988.243. Rochette 1996.100. Barney 2001.4–6. In describing the Atarantes, Herodotus distinguishes the category of proper names of individual persons from that of ethnic names (4.184.1).

[12] See e.g Thucydides 3.82.4–5; Plato *Cratylus* 411d–421b.

[13] See esp.4.65.2, ταύτην ἀνδραγαθίην λέγοντες.

[14] Hartog 1988.237–238.

Questioning Greek knowledge

In glosses attached to proper names of persons or places that appear in the narrative, the narrator explains what *x* "means" or "is called" in the Greek language or by the Greeks.[15] When the Greek name is clearly just an alternative to the original, the gloss represents the reverse of those passages in the *Iliad* that mention side by side the divine and the human name of a person or place as, for example, "the one the gods call Briareus, and all men Aigaion."[16] In Homer there are, practically speaking, no foreign languages; the main cultural divide is that which separates gods from mortals. When Homer translates words used by the gods, it occurs in a vacuum; this shows the only relatively privileged nature of the poet's relationship with the divine world. The narrator of the *Histories*, by contrast, is at home in the setting to which the unfamiliar name belongs (a distant but human setting, after all). Not only does he know, he also regularly uses the foreign names as an integral part of his history of cultures. Because the Greek counterpart is derivative or mistaken, it appears in the text only once, as a point of reference:[17]

---

[15] *Dunatai* (δύναται) is the clearest marker of a translation (Chamberlain 1999.275). But with formulae of the type "x in such and such a language is y" or "such and such a people call such and such a thing x," it is not always easy to tell whether translation or name replacement is intended. See e.g 3.26.1: "the city of Oasis" among the Ammonians, "a place which is called in Greek (κατὰ Ἑλλήνων γλῶσσαν) 'Islands of the Blessed'." Is the Greek denomination an entirely new invention? Or is it supposed to represent the translation of "Oasis" (on the real etymology of which, see Asheri 1990.243–244 and How and Wells 1928.1.262–263) or of some other local name?

[16] *Iliad* 1.403–404; see also 2.813–814 (human name Batieia, i. e. "Hill of the Thicket"/divine name "Tomb of Myrine"); 20.74 (divine name Xanthos/human name Scamander). The type of *dinumia* at 14.291, where the gloss concerns what we would call a common noun and records the double name of a type bird (divine name *khalkis*/human name *kymindis*), is only paralleled to a limited extent by the crocodile gloss in Herodotus (2.69.3, quoted below, p. 55). On Homeric translations, see Güntert 1921; Lazzeroni 1957; Watkins 1970; Strauss Clay 1972, who also cites the parody of the Iliadic practice in *Phaedrus* 252c; Kraus 1987.27–28. We should add Homer's explanation of the term "ichor" in *Iliad* 5.339–342. For translations in the *Odyssey*, see below, pp. 52–53. Homeric "divine" names are "charged," semantically marked, Greek words. Watkins 1970.2–3.

[17] This obviously does not apply to divinities that both Greeks and barbarian peoples worship, but by different names (see above, p. 31 and note 5); in such cases Herodotus uses either denomination. Another exception, when it is the Greek rather than the foreign name that Herodotus always uses in the narrative, occurs at 4.6.2: "The common name of all is *Skoloti* from the name of their king; but the Greeks call them Scyths." The text has been found unsatisfactory because the king in the story is named Kolaxais (see Macan 1889.1.4 for possible solutions). Skoloti may have actually been the name only of the autochthonous, non-nomadic tribes living west of the Borysthenes, who were subjected by the incoming Royal nomads (cf.

> The Greeks call also the Budini "Geloni," but they are wrong (οὐκ
> ὀρθῶς).
>
> 4.109.1
>
> Candaules, whom the Greeks call Myrsilus, was the king of Sardis . . .
>
> 1.7.2

In the first case the Greek name reveals insufficiently detailed ethnographic knowledge, since the half-Greek Geloni live in the territory of the Budini but are entirely dissimilar from them in origin, appearance, language, and customs.[18] The second gloss implies that the Greek name, however people came up with it, does not legitimately replace the Lydian consensus about one of their kings.[19] Naming historical figures, places, and peoples—and doing so with the utmost accuracy—is a fundamental aspect of Herodotus' task.[20]

The names by which the Greeks call foreign peoples and places are sometimes based on their own perception that the original names represent Greek words:

> the river which the Scythians call *Porata* and the Greeks *Pyretos*.
>
> 4.48.2

4.20,110). Kothe 1969.37–40. Notations on how peoples other than the Greeks call a foreign ethnic group occur e.g. at 7.63, 64.2, 72.1. For cases when Herodotus only mentions what "the Greeks call" a *foreign* object, personage, place, or people without objection and without giving a local or more correct term, see 2.15.3 ("what the Ionians call the Delta"), 2.112.1 (Proteus), 4.8.2 (Erythea), 4.33.3 (Hyperborean girls Hyperoche and Laodice), 4.199.1 (region of Cyrene called the Hills), and 2.105 (Sardonic linen; see end of note 19 below). The Greeks are also probably the name-givers at 2.125.1 ("stairs" or "platforms" of a pyramid). For Panhellenic expressions in general (what "the Greeks call so and so"), see above, p. 14 and note 36.

[18] See above, p. 25. Cf. 1.72.1 (with its counterpart at 7.72.1) and 7.63 where two different people are "called Syrians by the Greeks."

[19] According to Evans 1985, Myrsilus (from the Hittite *Mursilis*) may have been the right name for the Lydian king, but in Greek it became identical to that of the famous tyrant of Mytilene berated by Alcaeus, and to Herodotus it probably sounded too Greek. Candaules is authentic Lydian and perhaps a cult title of Hermes and of Heraclid kings. See Pedley 1974. A somewhat different case where Herodotus "corrects" a possibly accurate Greek conventional term for something foreign occurs at 2.105: "the Colchian linen is called 'Sardonikos' by the Greeks, while that from Egypt is called 'Egyptian'." The Greek name obscures the Colchian provenience of the first type of linen, which for Herodotus constitutes proof of the common origin of Egyptians and Colchians. Though the connection with Colchis may actually be encoded in the name *Sardonikos* (Lloyd 1988.26), neither the narrator nor his audience would have been aware of this.

[20] Campos Daroca 1992.83. Cf. for example Herodotus' caution when he gives the Bias/Pittacus alternative (1.27.2), and his statement about learning the names of the 300 at Thermopylae, though he will not include these in his narrative (7.224.1).

Mardonius . . . then sends against the Greeks the whole Persian cavalry led by <u>Masistios</u>, a man of great renown among the Persians, whom the Greeks call <u>Makistios</u>.

9.20

Pyretos, 'the Fiery One', applied to a river in Scythia, seems to show that the Greeks find any meaning preferable to no meaning at all.[21] On the other hand, *Makistios*, 'Tall Man', is analogous to many Greek renditions of foreign names that Herodotus normally uses as authentic;[22] it refers to physical characteristics and suggests magnificence, as Persian names normally do (1.139); and it coincides with Herodotus' description of this particular Persian general as an imposing figure.[23] But also the form *Makistios*, like *Pyretos*, is attributed to the Greeks so that it is not clear from the point of view of the text that either one represents an accurate translation rather than a Greek distortion of the original name.

This brings us to Herodotus' ambivalent attitude toward phonetic resemblances between barbarian languages and Greek. Herodotus has his own special sense of the occasional, mysterious transparency of foreign languages.[24] But he is also critical of the Greeks' unreflective response to barbarian names and the deafness they display to forms of speech not their own. To the Greek claim that the first king of Cyrene was named "Battus" because he stammered (from Greek *battarizō*), the narrator objects that, on the other hand: "in Libyan *battos* means 'king' (*basileus*)."[25] For Herodotus phonetic similarity is not always a guide to correct and complete interpretation, just as irreducible difference does not preclude meaning.

---

[21] Cf. Strabo 11.11.5 and 11.14.13 for Greek interpretations of names of foreign rivers. Campos Daroca 1992.111.

[22] E.g. Artaphrenes (5.25) suggesting *artiphrōn* (ἀρτίφρων) 'sound of mind' transliterates *Artafarna*. Hollmann 1998.131. See the list in Armayor 1978 with folk-etymologies; Georges 1994.53 and note 30.

[23] 9.25.1. How and Wells 1928.II.294. Chamberlain 1999.277.

[24] On transparency, see Chamberlain 1999.276–278. Cf. above, p. 12 and note 28; below, pp. 48–50.

[25] 4.155.2 (see below, pp. 79–83). On the real etymology, see Masson 1976 who argues that Herodotus is mistaken and the name, found in other parts of Greece, is really Greek and derives from *battarizō* (βατταρίζω). See also the Perinthian Greeks' obliviousness to the non-Greek meaning of *Paion* at 5.1.2–3 (below, pp. 69–70).

Names as *logoi* and *muthoi*

The Greek denominations Pyretos and Makistios illustrate the tendency to make a name say something about its object—to turn an *onoma* into a *logos*.[26] The substitution of sounds or letters that create these descriptive names is part of a current procedure in the Greek etymologies produced by poets, philosophers, Homeric commentators, Sophists, and other types of critics. Though most of the specific evidence is lost, we still have numerous examples from Homer and Hesiod to the fifth century and beyond.[27] Most remarkably, in Plato's *Cratylus* Socrates treats his interlocutors to a long agonistic display of etymologies in which he outdoes contemporary practitioners at their own game.[28] The etymologist's work consists in relating a proper name or common noun to other words so as to discover the name's deep content.[29] This may produce unexpected results and often requires slight (or not so slight) phonetic changes of the *Poretos/Pyretos* kind, as when Plato's Socrates derives the name Atreus from the adjective *ateros* 'ruinous'.[30]

Herodotus' familiarity with the etymologizing activity of his time is clear when he derives the Greek or "Ancient Pelasgian" word *theoi* from the root -θε- (*the-*) 'to settle' (2.52.1). The *Cratylus* contains many etymologies of this sort.[31] As far-fetched as they may seem to us, they were designed to elicit in the audience a retrospective sense of recognition and discovery as well as admiration for the ingenuity of the speaker, who was able to reveal the inner meaning of words.[32]

[26] On names as *logoi*, cf. e.g. Plato *Cratylus* 396a.

[27] E.g. *Theogony* 197–201; *Iliad* 22.506; *Odyssey* 19.406–409, cf. 1.62, 5.340, 423, 9.275. Forbes 1933.105–106; Stanford 1952; Nagy 1976; Kraus 1987.30–41, 136–146; Peradotto 1990 esp. 94–170; Baxter 1992.113n30. For the practice among early Greek natural philosophers to base physical theories on word etymologies, see Lloyd 1966.71. Heraclitus DK 48, for example, connects *biós* (βιός 'bow'), the weapon that brings death, to *bíos* (βίος 'life') to signify the doctrine of the coincidence of opposites. See Kahn 1979.201 and see also Heraclitus DK 32 and 56.

[28] *Cratylus* 391b–421e. For the notion of "agonistic display," see Barney 2001.60–80, who recognizes the humorous tone of the section but rejects the notion of parody supported by Baxter 1992.86–163. See also Kretzmann 1971; Levin 1995; 1997.46–50; Sedley 1998.

[29] Barney 2001.49–50. Cf. Barney 1992.107–163.

[30] *Cratylus* 395b–c. Socrates often mentions that in order to decode names one must perceive the phonetic transformations that have occurred in the language: 399a–b, 414b–d, 418b–419b. Baxter 1992.57–58.

[31] Thus at *Cratylus* 397c–d, the word θεοί is said to derive from the constant motion of the sun, moon, earth, stars, and sky, which represented the only divinities recognized in primitive Greece. On Herodotus 2.52.1, see above, p. 12.

[32] Barney 2001.71–72. Sedley 1998.142.

Herodotus, however, mainly etymologizes barbarian names for which he does not attempt to exploit a resemblance or relation to Greek:

> This spring is located at the border between the ploughmen-Scythians and the Alazones. The name of the spring and of the place whence it flows is in Scythian (Σκυθιστί) *Exampaios* and in Greek (κατὰ ... τὴν Ἑλλήνων γλῶσσαν) Sacred Ways.
>
> 4.52.3

The translation of the name and the elements of which it is composed here remains unverifiable. One must trust the word and linguistic expertise of the narrator, who has been at the site, talked to the natives, and learned the local names (4.81.2–6; cf. 4.52.1).[33]

Etymology makes a proper name reveal something about the importance, history, or attributes of the object to which it refers or, more precisely, it reflects the name-givers' perceptions of all these things. Foreign local names, unlike what "the Greeks call" some distant reality, provide an insider's view. Thus, in reference to the Egyptian troops who rebelled against Psammetichus and went over to the Ethiopian king after a particularly long service at the southern border of Egypt, the Greek term is the "Deserters" (αὐτόμολοι). In Egyptian, however,

> the name of these "Deserters" is *Asmakh*, and this word in Greek means "Those who stand at left of the king."
>
> τοῖσι δὲ αὐτομόλοισι τούτοισι οὔνομά ἐστι Ἀσμάχ, δύναται δὲ τοῦτο τὸ ἔπος κατὰ τὴν Ἑλλήνων γλῶσσαν οἱ ἐξ ἀριστερῆς χειρὸς παριστάμενοι βασιλεῖ.
>
> 2.30.1

The Egyptian name, *ounoma*, is called an *epos*, that is to say, an "utterance" or *logos* which tells a more complicated story than "deserters" or any other single word can express in Greek.[34] It also appears to reflect the point of view of these

---

[33] As it happens, Herodotus' translation of *Exampaios* has been given some credit. See Macan 1895.1.36; Corcella 1993.174–175. Foreign etymologies are relatively infrequent in other texts. See e.g. the etymology of the name of the Mysians from the Lydian name for a kind of beech-tree, in Xanthus the Lydian *FGrHist* 765 F 15. Thucydides gives the etymology of Zancle, the ancient name of Messina, "so called by the Sicels because the place is shaped like a sickle, and the Sicels call the sickle *zanklon*" (6.4.5). Cf. also Hell. *FGrHist* 4 F 111 (and F 71 for a Greek etymology of a foreign name).

[34] On the meaning of *epos* in Herodotus as an authoritative, coded, or otherwise significant utterance that is substantially, if not formally, equivalent to more than a single word, see Hollmann 2000, esp. 221–222 for this passage. Cf. also above, pp. 31–32 and note 10.

soldiers, whose discontent for their second-class position in Egypt caused them to resettle in Ethiopian lands.[35] Similarly, the Scythian name for the Amazons, once translated by components, describes the warrior character of this culture in a more direct and perhaps more truthful way than their name in Greek:

> The Scythians call the Amazons *Oiorpata*, and this name means in Greek (δύναται ... κατὰ Ἑλλάδα γλῶσσαν) "Mankillers" (ἀνδρο-κτόνοι); for they call "man" *oior*, and "kill" *pata*.
>
> 4.110.1[36]

What the etymology of a name reveals does not of course always constitute factual truth. Descriptive proper names, like the *logoi* the narrator reports, are only as reliable as the cultural knowledge they reflect. Thus the name of the so-called *Arimaspoi*, which is Scythian and means "One-Eyed" ("for the Scythians call 'one' *arima* and 'eye' *spou*" 4.27), merely testifies to the Scythian belief, based on unverified reports obtained from the neighboring Issedones, in the existence of a people of one-eyed men at the Northern extremities of the earth.[37] The narrator, however, rejects that claim (3.116). Comparable cases of uncorroborated *logoi* on the Greek side include, for example, the uncertain tradition on the Hyperboreans, 'Men Beyond the North Wind' (4.32–36.1), and the invention (verb *heuriskein*) of the river Ocean by Homer and Hesiod or some earlier poet.[38] Herodotus specifically talks about the invention of the *ounoma* 'name' of Ocean (2.23), pointing not so much to the word as a

[35] Cf. Diodorus Siculus 1.67; Strabo 16.4.8. For the controversy of whether *Asmakh* might actually derive from an Egyptian word for "left," see Lloyd 1976.128–129.

[36] Hartog 1980.240. The Greeks interpreted their own term "Amazon" as meaning "breast-less," or at least "lacking one breast"; this resulted in reports about their alleged custom of cauterizing the right breast for the sake of freedom of movement in handling weapons (Hellanicus, *FGrHist* 4 F 45; Hippocrates *Airs, Waters and Places* 17; Diodorus 2.45.3); Tyrrell 1984.49. In Herodotus, the Amazons look boyish from a distance, but a closer look apparently reveals nothing abnormal about their breasts (4.111.1). On the Amazons, see further below, pp. 72–73.

[37] On the scientific value of Herodotus' etymology, see Macan 1895.1.18. Corcella 1993.256. According to Chamberlain 1999.279, Herodotus is suggesting the transparency of the second element *spou* as the reverse of *ōps* in a compound of the type of *Kuklōps*. Explainable peoples' names follow either the descriptive model (*Arimaspoi, Melankhlainai, Androphagoi*) or the eponymic model. Campos Daroca 1992.91–92.

[38] For Herodotus' rejection of Ocean, see 2.23, 2.21, 4.2, 4.36.2. Factual information transmitted by poets is suspect in Herodotus. The existence of the river Eridanus flowing into the North Sea is rejected on the basis of its Greek *name*, which reveals it was "made up by some poet" (3.115.1–2). For the Hyperboreans, the main authorities are, beside the Delians (4.33.1), the Greek poets Homer and Hesiod (4.32). Romm 1989. Similarly, the fictional existence of the *Arimaspoi* is maintained by a poet, Aristeas of Proconnesus, who wrote an epic about them which featured the Hyperboreans as well (4.13). Asheri 1990.333–334.

phonetic and graphic entity as to the idea it communicates of a river that encircles the earth.[39] While in the case of the gods one cannot object to their human "names"—meaning, again, the conceptual image people have of each of them—"Ocean" is ascribed to the physical world and cannot be treated as irrefutable. In the absence of corroboration, it is an empty name and a false *logos*. The narrator calls it a *muthos* 'myth'.

When it comes to the description of the earth, Greek scientific theorizing meets mythology through the process of naming. Herodotus criticizes the abstract subdivision of the earth in Ionian maps in the same breath as the choice of "Asia," "Libya," and "Europe" as the continents' names:

> I cannot understand for what reason, since the earth is one, there should be three names (*ounomata*) placed on it, deriving their denomination (*epōnumias*) from women ... and I cannot find out the names of those who made the subdivision, nor the sources from which they took these denominations (*epōnumias*).
>
> 4.45.2

Libya is supposed to have been a woman native of the land she named, and Asia is named after the wife of Prometheus—unless "Asia" is a Lydian name, derived from that of Asies, the son of Cotys. As for Europe, no one knows whether it is surrounded by water—that is to say, it is not clear that it is a separate land mass, worthy of its own name in the first place. Moreover, if this region is called after the Tyrian princess abducted to Crete, the eponymic model again makes no sense.

Herodotus' rejection of the role of these mythical women in geography parallels his skepticism in the proem towards the historical relevance of the abductions of women in the Persian and Phoenician narratives of the proem (1.1–5).[40] But while Herodotus' *logos* needs Helen or Io as little as it needs Ocean, it cannot do away with the continents. "Enough with these matters," the narrator says, τοῖσι νομιζομένοισι χρησόμεθα—"we will continue to use the customary names" (4.45.5).

Metaphorical names

Descriptive names sometimes represent reality in metaphorical terms, with neither claims to realism nor intention to deceive. A pleasant spot in the

---

[39] See above on the "names" of the gods, pp. 11–13 and note 22.

[40] Campos Daroca 1992.113–114.

middle of the desert is appropriately named in Greek "Islands of the Blessed" (3.26.1). The name of a temple in Egypt "of foreign Aphrodite" is charming but misleading. Luckily the *histōr* understands that it really denotes Helen, who is honored in Egypt since her stay in that land while the war was raging at Troy on her behalf (2.112.2). In names, as in oracular utterances, metaphors need to be interpreted as such to be informative about their referents or creators. The *histōr* is an expert *hermēneus* 'interpreter' in the linguistic, as in the religious, area.[41] The Scythians say that to the north of their country, beyond the territory of their immediate neighbors, the earth and air are all full of feathers that impede progress and visibility (4.7.3). In his subsequent account of bitter Scythian winters, Herodotus steps in to offer his opinion (*gnōmē*) about these feathers. They clearly refer to snow flakes, which fall in abundance in Northern Europe and which resemble (οἶκε) feathers, as everyone who has seen snow knows (4.31.1):

> It is therefore *in a figurative sense* (εἰκάζοντας), I think (δοκέω), that <u>the Scythians and their neighbors call the snow "feathers."</u>

> 4.31.2

The Scythian report does not point to a fabulous land where feathers fall out of the sky nor does it indicate that the Scythians consider snow and feathers as one and the same.[42] The length of Herodotus' explanation and the triple grammatical first person show that the narrator is interpreting barbarian speech that was, or could be, misunderstood in the translation.[43] Linguistic metaphor is among the Scythians a form of economy well suited to their simple culture, as are their rude expressions: "Go weep!" (κλαίειν λέγω, 4.127.4) is a Scythian *rhēsis*, says Herodotus.[44] Similarly, the Spartans are colloquially abrupt, call an arrow "spindle," and economize on words.[45]

Metaphorical names lend themselves to misinterpretation or even political instrumentalization. According to Herodotus, the wife of the cowherd

---

[41] The analogy between oracles and names emerges from the references to the role of divine inspiration in namegiving or the interpretation of names in Plato's *Cratylus* (396d, 428c). On Herodotus' ability to interpret metaphors, see also below, pp. 67–69.

[42] On Herodotus' use of *eikazō* (εἰκάζω) 'liken' to indicate a deliberate metaphor cf. 2.69.3, 9.34.1 and especially 7.162.2. Munson 2001.83n114.

[43] As have some modern scholars: see Benardete's reference to "the Scythians' failure to see a likeness as likeness" (Benardete 1969.100–110).

[44] Corcella 1984.83, 94–96; 1993.258, 325. Other Scythian metaphorical names appear at 4.52.1 and 59.2 (below, p. 44). For the peculiarities of Scythian communication, see also West 1988; Munson 2001.114–115.

[45] See Thucydides 4.40.2: τὸν ἄτρακτον, λέγων τὸν οἰστόν. See above, pp. 17–18 and note 52.

who raised Cyrus, "was named <u>Kyno</u> (i.e. 'Dog') in Greek, and in Median <u>Spako</u>; for the Medes call a bitch <u>spako</u>" (1.110.1). This verbal correspondence later allowed Cyrus' real parents to spread the tale that he had been suckled by a bitch "so that the Persians might think even more that the child was saved by the will of the gods" (1.122.3).[46] Already Hecataeus had recognized the potential of language for creating false *logoi*. When he explains that Cerberus was really a serpent metaphorically named "the hound of Hades" (*FGrHist* 1 F 27), his rationalizing critique of the myth uses a procedure similar to that of Herodotus in the story of Spako, only in reverse.

Correct names

That names, like *logoi*, can be misleading and that one cannot always attain knowledge through them are aspects of Herodotus' critical stance toward what people conventionally say and think. For him names entail conceptual representations (as the names of the gods), but they are autonomous from the sphere of concrete facts. Some names exist with no corresponding reality (e.g., Ocean and *Arimaspoi* 'One-Eyed Men').[47] A single name can denote two different referents,[48] just as one thing can legitimately be called by different names.[49] Conversely, not all that exists in nature has a name or a good enough name, nor always the same name over time.[50] Symbolic of the flexible degree of dependence between a thing and its identity (or identification) through naming are the streams of the vale of Thessaly that flow into the Peneus river:

[46] The dog was an animal sacred to the Medes (see 1.140 and How and Wells 1928.1.108), and the name of the cowherd, Mithradatas, is similarly connected to the god Mithra. Historically, the legend about the supernatural childrearing of the exposed Cyrus must have preceded the "human" version which Herodotus reports as more accurate.

[47] For a political instance of "empty" name, see the "*so-called* tomb" (καλεόμενος τάφος) of the Aeginetans built at Plataea just for show, and containing no bones (9.85.3).

[48] As Cambyses finds out with the two Smerdis, similar in body as well as in name, and the two Ecbatana (3.61.2; 64).

[49] See e.g. the Linus song (2.79). On Prodicus' study of synonymy in Greek, see Aristotle *Topics* 112b 22. Classen 1976.231–234.

[50] E.g. 4.184.1: the Atarantes have no personal names (i.e., no names exist for individuals that nevertheless exist). Absurd names are for Herodotus those of the continents (4.45.2–4); see above, p. 39; below, pp. 43, 55, 66. People attribute different meanings to a name ("Egypt," 2.15.3). Places and peoples frequently change their names (e.g., the Athenians, 8.44.2; Calliste/Thera, 4.147.4). An obvious case of adventitious names is represented by the animal names Cleisthenes gives to the new Sicyonian tribes (5.68.1). On the instability of the meaning of abstract words, see Thucydides, 3.82.4–8.

41

the Peneus overwhelms the other rivers with its name (τῷ οὐνόματι) and renders them nameless (ἀνωνύμους). They say that in ancient times, when the vale and outlet did not yet exist, these rivers did not have names (οὔτε ὀνομάζεσθαι) as now, but still used to flow no less than now.

7.129.3

But Herodotus' awareness that objects are separable from names leaves room for cases when an intimate, even mysterious connection appears to exist between the two. It is at least possible that, when confronted with something that can be documented in other ways, one might be able to recognize it in its name. This attitude is consistent with the purpose of fifth-century Greek etymology, which does not investigate historical linguistic roots and original meanings, but rather tests the appropriateness of a name to its object.[51] Greek interest in the relation between language and the world is in turn tied to the issue we have already mentioned of whether language itself exists "by nature" (φύσει) or "by convention" (νόμῳ, συνθήκῃ, or ὁμολογίᾳ). If an individual word is a natural feature of its referent—for example, the *bekós* of 2.2.3 in Psammetichus' interpretation of his experiment—it will suit it perfectly.[52] Thus, in Plato's *Cratylus*, Socrates suggests that the names Homer mentions as belonging to the language of the gods must of course be naturally right (*Cratylus* 391d–e). If, on the other hand, signifiers are chosen by convention, one may argue that they are arbitrary, more or less well crafted, or replaceable by other labels.

In the *Cratylus*, the homonymous character theorizes that names and things are strictly linked. In his view, a word that does not naturally belong to the object to which the speaker refers is not a name at all, but mere noise, or the name of something else (383b; 429b–430a). His opponent Hermogenes is a radical conventionalist who maintains that any name by which one chooses to call something is just as good as another. Socrates mediates between these two positions. On the side of convention, he maintains that naming is a human activity and therefore subject to error.[53] Even the most expressive of names cannot teach us about essences. We must learn about things first through the things themselves because by investigating their nature through names we are likely to be deceived (436a–440e). At the same time, independently of what a name expresses, convention plays an important role in communication. The

---

[51] Barney 2001.51.

[52] See above, pp. 19–23.

[53] *Cratylus* 429a–431e, 433d–e; cf. 400d–401a. The distinction between the descriptive and the prescriptive aspects of the argument is emphasized by Baxter 1992.9–12.

name of Socrates' interlocutor Hermogenes, for example, is not very suitable, since this individual is no "son of Hermes," in either a literal or a metaphorical sense.[54] The word *sklērotēs* is also imperfect, though on different grounds: it is supposed to mean "hardness," yet the "l" sound it contains rather imitates softness. But if everyone uses these names to indicate certain referents, they legitimately represent their names and are essential for fulfilling the proper task of all names, that is to say, instruction.[55] Socrates' argument here recalls Herodotus' declaration that he will refer to the continents by their customary names (τοῖσι νομιζομένοισι) even though he finds them unsatisfactory.[56]

On the other side of the issue, Socrates indulges Cratylus' view by verifying at great length that actual names in Greek are significant by virtue of their resemblance to their referents. Like Herodotus, he considers it desirable for a word to bear a natural relation to the thing named. Leaving aside its more profound philosophical repercussions for Plato's thought, the argument in the *Cratylus* testifies to a culture-wide way of looking at language and names. Both proper and common names say something meaningful about their objects—or so they should, to be good names—and it is normal to try and evaluate how well they do this.[57] A name that is appropriately imposed or used is considered "correct": *orthos* and derivatives are key terms in fifth-century discussions about language.[58] In the etymological section of the *Cratylus*, for example, Socrates argues that of the two names of Hector's son, Scamandrius and Astyanax, Homer attributes a higher degree of correctness (*orthotēs*) to the latter, since "Lord of the city" is appropriate for the son of the sole defender of Troy.[59]

In Herodotus we have already seen the adverb *orthōs* used to reject as "not right" the practice of referring to an object the name belonging to another object (4.109.1: "Geloni" is not the right name of the Budini, but of a different people). Elsewhere Herodotus praises the *orthotēs* of a foreign name that appears to represent accurately the thing to which it refers. In these cases etymological analogy reveals to the *histōr* a correspondence between the name

---

54 429b–c; Hermogenes is represented as the direct opposite of Hermes: he is apparently not successful in business (383b–384c) and not a good contriver of speech (407e–408b). It is ironically fitting, of course, that a proponent of the absolutely arbitrary nature of language should bear such an ill-suited name.

55 *Cratylus* 388b–c; 434b–435d.

56 4.45.5. See above, p. 39.

57 See e.g. Burkert 1985.126–127; Baxter 1992.95–96.

58 For the different shades of meaning of terms such as *orthoepeia* and *orthotēs*, according to Protagoras, Prodicus, and Democritus, see Classen 1976; Thomas 2000.230.

59 *Cratylus* 392b–e, in reference to *Iliad* 22.506.

and its object that can be verified by other means: "This lake is rightly (*orthōs*) called 'mother of Hypanis'" (4.52.1).[60] The "mother of Hypanis" is a great body of water from which the Scythian river Hypanis flows.[61] Somewhat like "feathers" for "snow," this Scythian metaphor corresponds to a hypothetical eyewitness's perception of the referent. We cannot be sure this time that the idiom in fact translates a foreign word, but given the entirely Scythian context of the gloss, it comes across as such.[62]

In the following gloss, the narrator exploits the transparency of the foreign name and implicitly relates the Scythian name "Papaios" to the Greek word *pappas* 'father': "In Scythian (Σκυθιστί) Zeus is called, most correctly in my opinion (ὀρθότατα κατὰ γνώμην γε τὴν ἐμήν), *Papaios*" (4.59.2).[63] Nowhere else in the *Histories* does Herodotus etymologize, much less evaluate, the name of a divinity, whether in Greek or any other language.[64] Glosses that give the foreign equivalent of the name of a Greek god are normally incidental to descriptions of cult and contain no other comment.[65] Since the explanation of a name amounts to a *logos*, the fact that Herodotus does not explain divine names is consistent with his program of avoiding discussion of τὰ ... θεῖα τῶν ἀπηγημάτων οἷα ἤκουον ... ἔξω ἢ τὰ οὐνόματα αὐτῶν μοῦνον, 'the narratives I heard about the gods, except their *names* pure and simple' (2.3.2). "*Papaios*" is a unique case in which the name of a foreign divinity confirms his or her identification with one of the Olympians. The narrator corroborates the description conveyed by the name, signals his caution, and takes responsibility: 'at least in my opinion', κατὰ γνώμην γε τὴν ἐμήν.[66] According to the Scythians, Gaia is the wife of Zeus

---

[60] Outside of the linguistic sphere, *orthos* is part of Herodotus' vocabulary of corroboration. For *orthos* in reference to correct opinions, *logoi*, measurements and other data in Herodotus, Democritus, sophists and fifth-century medical writers, see Thomas 2000.228–235; as referring to correspondence in Herodotus, aside from the linguistic application of the term, see Darbo-Peschanski 1987.183.

[61] Cf. 4.86.4, where the statement that the *Palus Maeotis* is the "mother of Pontus" may have been suggested by an etymology of *Maiētis* (Μαιῆτις; perhaps the Greek rendition of a "transparent" Scythian word) from *maia* (μαῖα). Macan 1889.1.61–62. Corcella 1993.303.

[62] For other foreign words given in translation, see above, p. 31 and note 8.

[63] Macan 1895.1.40. Mora 1985.50–51.

[64] Divine names are an especially frequent object of etymology in other Greek texts. See e.g. *Cratylus* 395e–396d, 400d–409b. On Plutarch's Greek etymologies of Egyptian divine names in the *Isis and Osiris*, see Donadoni 1947.

[65] Linforth 1926.8. See above, p. 31 and note 5.

[66] Cf. the reservations made by Socrates in *Cratylus* 400d–401a: we do not know anything about the gods and their real names; we can only discuss the names by which we call them according to *nomos* and which men originally invented on the basis of human *doxa* ('opinion').

44

(4.59.1). This is peculiar to them, and equivalent to the different cultural beliefs of other nations (2.3.2).[67] But their name for Zeus, at any rate, shows signs of correctness, because it expresses what the Greek name expresses, the idea of life-giving, and this agrees with what the Greeks and many other peoples believe about the essential, patriarchal position of their main divinity.[68]

Herodotus' evaluation of the "rightness" of barbarian names is unparalleled in Greek literature. The contemporary fifth-century tendency to look at language and speech in terms of greater or lesser *orthotēs* seems in most cases to have focused on Greek only, ignoring other languages.[69] The *Cratylus* provides a partial exception to this rule, because it explicitly maintains that barbarian *onomata* may be correct. According to Cratylus, "the *standard* of correctness (*orthotēs*) in names is the same for all men, both Greek and barbarians" (383a–b). Socrates approves of this position and brings it one step further: the Greek and the barbarian name for the same thing can both be right, just as two or more completely different Greek names can have the same *dunamis* ('meaning/force') and an equal degree of correctness (Hector, 'Holder/Ruler', and Astyanax, 'Lord of the City', for example).[70]

The concessions to the legitimacy of barbarian names in the *Cratylus* must have been controversial among contemporary Greeks. If we compare them with the passage in the *Statesman* that rejects as lopsided the chauvinistic distinction between Greeks and barbarians, Plato's position appears rooted in a polemic somewhat similar to that of Herodotus.[71] The regard for foreign languages in the *Cratylus*, in contrast to the *Histories*, remains entirely theoretical. In practice, Cratylus regards Greek as correct for the most part and makes no similar claim for any other language.[72] Socrates,

---

[67] For a discussion of 2.3.2, see Munson 2001.163–166. Thomas 2000.280 proposes a different interpretation.

[68] For the etymology of Zeus (Ζεύς) from *zēn* (ζῆν) 'live', see *Cratylus* 396a–b and, implicitly, Aeschylus *Suppliants* 584–585.

[69] As Burkert observes (1985.126), the existence of different languages is not emphasized in Greek thought even by those who could have used it to bolster their argument against a theory of natural language (e.g. Democritus DK 68 B26).

[70] 389d4–390a2; 394a–c. In the case of the third character of the dialogue, Hermogenes, the idea of the validity of a barbarian name is of course implicit in his belief that the right name of a thing is whatever an individual or city wants to call it (384c8–385a5).

[71] 262c–263a. Miller 1980.20–24. Baxter 1992.15, 44–45 juxtaposes the *Statesman* and the *Cratylus* on this issue; Braund 1998.178n29 cites the passage from the *Statesman* in his discussion of Herodotus. See also below, p. 66. In *Protagoras* 341c a characteristic of barbarians seems to be the incorrect use of names.

[72] *Cratylus* 383a4–b2; Baxter 1992.136.

for his part, gives no example of foreign names showing that they are (or are not) correct. He considers Greek words only, either by deriving them from other Greek words (etymology) or, in the case of primary names, by analyzing their forms and sounds as vocal imitations of certain qualities inherent to their objects. When he cannot make sense of certain words by either method—as in the case, for example, of *pur* 'fire' and *hudōr* 'water'—he ironically adopts what he calls a clever expedient (*mēkhanē*): they are of barbarian derivation, possibly Phrygian.[73] It seems that since barbarian words are incomprehensible to the Greeks, incomprehensible Greek words must therefore be barbarian.

The conversation of philosophers in the *Cratylus* both transcends and reflects the unexamined assumptions of the general public. In the ethnic prejudice of the Greeks the word *barbaroi* denotes those who speak in an unintelligible way, and more specifically—since the word objectifies the subjective—the utterers of inarticulate and meaningless sounds.[74] This definition of the non-Greek seems almost to have provided the model for what Cratylus in the dialogue says about those who do not use the "right" and true names of things: they are not speakers but makers of noises, "like one banging on a cauldron" (*Cratylus* 430a5–6).

The narrator of the *Histories* is not, as we have seen, entirely immune from impressionistic descriptions of barbarian speech as pure sound,[75] but the evidence of his etymologies rather points in the other direction. The language of the primitive Scythians makes sense and has its own brand of expressiveness. Barbarians, like Greeks, can be competent crafters of names.

Nomen omen

Within the broader issue of correctness, personal names occupy a special place. In Euripides' *Trojan Women*, Hecuba exclaims at one point that Aphrodite is *rightly* (*orthōs*) named from *aphrosunē*, 'folly', as she recognizes from her own experience the goddess and her destructive work in her name.[76] Human names were given with the intention to communicate something, to classify

---

[73] 409a5–410a5, 416a, 425e. Lejeune 1940–1948.49–50; Rochette 1996.96–97.

[74] See above, Introduction, pp. 1–3.

[75] 4.183.4. See above, p. 25.

[76] *Trojan Women* 989–990. Guthrie 1969.207n2. Cf. the famous Ἑλένας, ἕλανδρος, ἑλέπτολις of Aeschylus *Agamemnon* 689–690.

its bearer or endow him with an auspicious symbol.[77] In Herodotus, Persian names are important indicators of status; by contrast, the nameless Atarantes must have seemed, from a Greek point of view, impoverished indeed.[78] Greek parents named their children after an ancestor, the family's hereditary craft, characteristics or accomplishments of the father (or sometimes of the mother), or with theophoric names—like the misapplied "Hermogenes" of the *Cratylus* or, for that matter, "Herodotus."[79] In historical times, at least, it was rare for a person to have a name designed to characterize him individually.[80] If a name retrospectively turned out to suit special features of its adult owner, the correspondence was a sort of revelation.[81] As soon as Herodotus mentions the Athenian statesman Aristides (the form of the name is a patronymic: "son of . . ."), he emphasizes his well-known honesty and calls him *aristos* (8.79.1).[82] The text of the *Histories* also alludes to the profound symbolic importance of the name of Leonidas, 'son of Lion', which so perfectly and mysteriously encapsulates the essence of the warrior-king of Thermopylae.[83] Similarly, Herodotean characters pay attention to each other's names.[84]

[77] For the intentionality and classificatory function of names, see Morpurgo Davies 2000.20–25. Campos Daroca 1992.114–122.

[78] 1.139; 4.184.2–3. See above, p. 26. Hornblower (2000.134) counts 940 personal names in Herodotus as opposed to 473 in Thucydides.

[79] Sulzberger 1926; Nagy 1979.146n2; Svenbro 1993.69–79. In Herodotus, the father of the Spartan Archias was named Samius after his grandfather, who had died at Samos (3.55.2). For theophoric names, see Parker 2000.

[80] Sulzberger 1926.399–400 gives examples from epic where, on the contrary, this type of name is frequent (e.g. *Telegonus* 'Born faraway'). In Herodotus, names deliberately imposed by the parents to describe a child include *Oeolycus* 'Lamb among Wolves', derived from an utterance, or *epos*, of his father Theras (4.149.1; see Hollmann 2000, note 24) and, according to the Greeks, *Battus* 'Stammerer' (4.155; see above, p. 35 and below, pp. 82–83).

[81] For the *omen-nomen* ideology in other ancient cultures, see Cardona 1976.133–139. On the connotative function of proper names, with references to modern philosophical theory and its application to the names of the *Odyssey*, see Peradotto 1990.94–119. For the extent to which Thucydides reflects contemporary interest in proper names, see Hornblower 1992.151–154; 2000.136–137.

[82] Apparently a common pun, even in Aristides' lifetime; see Plutarch *Aristides* 3.

[83] 7.225, cf. 125. Immerwahr 1966.260–261; Georges 1994.141–142; Munson 2001.246. See also Demaratus (6.63.3). Other cases in Immerwahr 1967.294–295; Campos Daroca 1992.122–134; Harrison 1998, note 145; Chamberlain 1999, note 43; Hollmann 1998.126–130; Hornblower 2000.134–135. According to the same principle, homonymy may be a sign of substantial similarities between the name-bearers. See e.g. especially 5.69.1 and 67.1 (Cleisthenes), arguably 2.100.2 (Nitocris), and 3.61–80 (Smerdis, with the added factor of the semantic transparency of the name, akin to *smerdaleos* [σμερδάλεος]); Armayor 1978.156; Chamberlain 1999.293.

[84] See 6.50.3 (Krios); 7.180 (Leon); 9.91 (Hegesistratus), discussed below.

Even more unexpected are those cases when a name turns out to describe, not its owner's permanent attributes, but that person's role in a particular historical context or from an outsider's viewpoint. At the time of the Greek land victory of Plataea, the name of a Samian herald persuades the Spartan king Leotychides to support with the fleet an Ionian revolt against Persia. This man made a long-winded speech, but Leotychides interrupted him.

> Either because he wanted to know in order to receive an omen, or by a chance brought about by god (κατὰ συντυχίην θεοῦ ποιεῦντος), Leotychides said: "Stranger from Samos, what is your name?" The other said, "Hegesistratus (i.e., 'Leader of the Army')." Cutting Hegesistratus short, in case he was about to add something else, Leotychides said: "I accept the omen, stranger from Samos."
>
> 9.91.1–2

The episode ironically characterizes Spartan religiosity, their standoffishness with strangers, and their dislike for long speeches.[85] But Herodotus' narrative suggests the fortuitous nature of Leotychides' question (κατὰ συντυχίην θεοῦ ποιεῦντος) and creates another omen with the pun involving *his* name: συντυχίην/Λεοτυχίδης.[86] The ominous meaning of the names of the men who will lead the Greeks to Mycale is later confirmed by the other divine signs predicting the victory.[87]

In Herodotus, foreign names can also be profoundly meaningful. The following gloss appears at the end of an important interpretive passage, where the narrator says that an unprecedented number of evils have befallen Greece during the generations of Darius, Xerxes, and Artaxerxes:

> In Greek these names mean (δύναται ... κατὰ Ἑλλάδα γλῶσσαν), <u>Darius</u> *Erxies* ('Doer'), <u>Xerxes</u> *Areios* ('Warrior'), <u>Artaxerxes</u> *Megas Areios* ('Great Warrior'). This is what the Greeks would correctly (*orthōs*) call these kings in their language.
>
> 6.98.3

The etymological note appeared so abrupt and unmotivated that editors used to excise it from the text, but all now recognize that it serves to confirm the preceding interpretation by bringing out the *nomen-omen* factor.[88]

---

[85] Cf. 1.152.1–2, 3.46 and 5.49–50. Notice Leotychides' double use of the address *xeine* (ξεῖνε; cf. above, p. 17 and note 50).

[86] Stadter 1992.792n29.

[87] 9.100–101. Munson 2001.194–195.

[88] Wood 1972.141–142n55; Stadter 1992.790; Harrison 1998; Chamberlain 1999.267–272.

Herodotus first identifies the earthquake of Delos at the time of the Persian crossing in 490 BC as a divine occurrence marking the inception of the evils that have plagued Greece in this period, partly as a result of the Persian invasion and partly on account of internal wars. Then he reports an old oracle that had predicted the earthquake. As a third order of signs, he inserts the passage cited above, with his translation of the mighty names that "name" the epoch. The context is prophetic as is the substance of the narrator's "beginning of evil" pronouncement.[89] Herodotus' etymologies have the mantic character of Leotychides' discovery of Hegesistratus' name and of the creation and interpretation of names as represented in Plato's *Cratylus*.

As Herodotus interprets the Persian names and creates original translations, his choice of Greek forms is nothing short of sensational. *Areios* is predominantly poetic, especially Homeric, and not elsewhere applied to persons in the *Histories*. *Erxies* is semantically transparent—formed on the root *erg-*, 'do'—but in the words of A. B. Cook, "excessively rare."[90] These forms, used instead of more ordinary Greek words, reveal that Herodotus is not simply translating in order to explain the verbal meaning of the names but is also making an effort to maintain intact the connotative qualities, or force (*dunatai*), of the Persian originals.

But there is more. Cook drew attention to a glaring similarity between Greek and Persian forms and proposed to emend the text into "*Darius Areios, Xerxes Erxies, Artaxerxes Megas Erxies* (or rather, *Karta Erxies*)." If we accept Cook's emendation, this is a straightforward, if especially creative, case of perceived transparency between a foreign language and Greek.[91] We are, however, faced with the problem of how a textual corruption of this sort could ever have occurred.[92] Chamberlain, who prefers to keep the *lectio difficilior*, argues that it is nevertheless unlikely that the echo of the original names in the rare Greek forms might have been produced unconsciously or by chance. The problem then becomes what the translator was thinking by interlacing phonetically similar forms from father to son.[93]

---

[89] Chamberlain 1999.271. Munson 2001.201–205.

[90] It occurs only in Archilochus fr. 62 Diehl. See *Etymologicum Magnum* 376, 52 ff. and Cook 1907. See also Wood 1972.141–142n55.

[91] See above, p. 12 and note 28. For other Persian personal names the Greeks evidently regarded as transparent, see above, p. 35, note 22.

[92] Cook 1907. His emendation is accepted by Stadter 1992.790 and tentatively Harrison 1998, ch. 4 "The imagined relationship between Greek and foreign languages."

[93] Chamberlain 1999.267–272; he is, as far as I know, the only one who has explored this problem.

According to Chamberlain, Herodotus has what he calls a "meta-rhythmic" view of translation. He applies to language the conception of the *rhusmos* (Attic *rhuthmos*) 'flowing shape', which Democritus attributes to the atoms, and he discovers a more hidden transparency in foreign languages by transposing individual letters, syllables, or entire words.[94] Herodotus says that the Phoenicians who imported the alphabet to Greece changed the shape (*rhuthmos*) of the letters when they changed their language from Phoenician to Greek.[95] Similarly, "Herodotean translation … deals with the *rhusmos* or synoptic shape of the word and, hence, with what other words it can be exchanged (*dunatai*)."[96]

Chamberlain's metarhythmic theory cannot be applied to all, or even most, of Herodotus' translations of foreign words. It complements, however, the evidence concerning Herodotus' views of transparency and, in this particular passage, it has the merit of maintaining both the integrity of the text and the meaningfulness of the formal aspects of Herodotus' translation. Herodotus the researcher (like the *histōr* as a character of the *Histories*) can choose how to interpret the evidence and whether to include it in his work, but he cannot deliberately distort or invent it. Faced with the information, for example, that the name of Darius has to do with activity and that of Xerxes with belligerence (and not the other way around or some other meaning), he allows his audience nevertheless to discover that there is a way, though not the most direct and obvious way, in which the Greek meaning of these Persian names is connected with how their sound and shape in the original language strikes a Greek speaker.[97] As it happens, the intertwining of the names through their translation into Greek symbolically enhances the idea that they are significant not individually but in a block: in Herodotus' interpretation of the earthquake of Delos, the three consecutive generations of kings define what is, from the point of view of the Greeks, a unitary period of history.[98]

The narrator's attempt to come up with the *right* names for these kings, only in Greek, is confirmed by the second sentence of the gloss, a retrospective conclusion which at first sight seems particularly redundant but which

---

[94] Chamberlain 1999.266–267, 282–286.

[95] 5.58, where we find both *rhuthmon* (ῥυθμόν) and *metaruthmisantes* (μεταρυθμίσαντες). Chamberlain 1999.266–267, 284.

[96] Chamberlain 1999.286.

[97] Herodotus' translations at 6.98.3, no matter how we switch them, are in reality wrong (Macan 1889.1.334; Stein 1894.3.195, How and Wells 1928.2.105, Legrand 1948.100, cf.1932.74); but this is, as usual, beside the point.

[98] Munson 2001.203–205.

corroborates his translation with the telltale *orthōs*. Often the Greeks ascribe to foreign people and things the wrong name, but here "this is what the Greeks would correctly (*orthōs*) call these kings in their language." Herodotus is not commenting on the correctness of the original barbarian names in this case (though that is surely implied),[99] but rather on that of the Greek words that interpret and translate them. These etymologies demonstrate that, if one takes due care, it is possible to translate certain names that belong to one *ethnos* correctly into the language of another *ethnos*, and produce a name that is *orthos*, i.e, one that describes the object as appropriately as the original does.

In the representation we derive from Herodotus' translations of barbarian names into Greek, all languages apparently work very much in the same way. Opaque foreign words (e.g. the Median for "dog") are apparently no more or less correct, arbitrary, or explainable than their Greek counterparts.[100] Foreign languages also include names that possess a varying degree of phonetic transparency from the point of view of a Greek listener, though a foreign name's resemblance to Greek does not invariably lead to a correct interpretation of its meaning. When words, simple or in combination and more or less transparent, are applied attributively to persons and places, they convey descriptions or definitions (*logoi*) which can be rendered into a Greek word or phrase possessing a degree of *orthotēs* in relation to their objects equal to that of the originals. Herodotus' etymological translations indicate that different languages are equivalent in worth and meaning, so that the narrator can make an unfamiliar world more familiar through translation.

Giving the "right" word

Another type of metalinguistic gloss provides a common noun designating a foreign object or institution for which the Greek language has no original name, or no adequate name, or no name at all.[101] In a few cases the gloss acknowledges a linguistic and material debt of the Greeks to a foreign culture (never the other way around). Thus the translation of the Greek

---

[99] The suggestion by Harrison 1998 (ch. 4, "The imagined relationship between Greek and foreign languages") that Herodotus may consider the Persian names "a distorted, corrupt version of Greek" is unjustified. Elsewhere in Herodotus native names are presented as the most accurate.

[100] In Greek these are regarded by Socrates of the *Cratylus* either as derived from a barbarian language or as "primary words" that imitate their objects phonetically rather than through representation (422a–d2).

[101] See R. Waterfield's glossary of foreign words in Herodotus in Dewald 1998.742–744.

word for the aromatic substance "ledanum—*which the Arabs call <u>ladanum</u>*" (3.112)—establishes that, since Arabia is the only land to produce this and other spices (3.107.1), the Greek name is based on the Arabic. In the course of the same description the narrator reminds his audience of the foreign origin of the Greek name of another spice collected in Arabia, "sticks, *which we call <u>cinnamon</u>, with a word we learned from the Phoenicians*" (3.111.2).[102]

Most of the foreign terms in these glosses, however, are opaque words for things that are unknown to the Greeks and have no name in Greek. These notations have an entirely different effect from the ones considered in the preceding section. Instead of giving a comforting sense of linguistic equivalence between barbarian and Greek, they imply an area of discrepancy. Rather than explaining, they make things more difficult. In these cases the *histōr* starts from a Greek word or expression, which by itself denotes the foreign phenomenon in an approximate way. He then makes the required linguistic adjustment by qualifying the Greek term with a description and gives the precisely accurate term, necessarily foreign. So, concerning the bituminous oil found in Ardericca of Cissia (by the way: we call it "petroleum"), Herodotus says: "this oil (ἔλαιον) ... *the Persians call it <u>rhadinakē</u>*: it is black and has a heavy smell."[103]

The discourse pattern is here similar to that of the cases of *mononumia* ('single-nameness') in the *Odyssey*. There is no human word to denote the plant with black root and white flower the gods call *moly* because men do not

---

[102] Greek-derived words in a foreign language are only mentioned in those cases when heroes give their (presumably Greek) names to foreign dynasties (e.g. 1.7.2). Non-linguistic debts incurred by the Greeks toward foreign countries are also reflected in language otherwise than through the borrowing of the foreign name of the thing, e.g. in the case of "Phoenician letters," a denomination which the narrator considers entirely "fair" (*dikaion*, not *orthon*: 5.58.2). The word *aigis* (αἰγίς), though Herodotus does not say it is of Libyan derivation, somehow proves to him that the aegis of Greek statues of Athena represents a Libyan borrowing (4.189.2). A lexical exchange among non-Greek cultures is noted in a gloss which recognizes the name of a people north of the Ister, the Syginnae, both in a noun used by a Celtic tribe north of Massalia and in one with different meaning used in Cyprus: "for the Ligyes north of Massalia <u>suginnae</u> are shopkeepers, and for the Cyprians that is the name for spears" (5.9.3).

[103] 6.119.4. The word *elaion* (ἔλαιον) normally means olive oil, as one can see from the restricted use of the word at 1.193.4. Benveniste 1966 surveys Persian words in Herodotus, distinguishing "borrowings," i.e., loan-words which will become part of the Greek language (often found for the first time in Herodotus), from Iranian words, like this one, which are reproduced as such in the text and are never incorporated into the Greek language. See also Harrison 1998, ch. 1 with notes 30 and 32. The distinction is not crucial for my purposes: when presented in a gloss, even a loan word counts as a genuine foreign word. We should notice, however, that genuine foreign words are more frequent in the ethnographic sections, while loan-words tend to appear especially in the historical narrative.

know the *phusis* of this plant.[104] Similarly, the lack of a Greek counterpart for *rhadinakē*, corresponds to a gap in the knowledge of the Greeks. The word *bekós* (2.2) can be immediately turned from Phrygian into the Egyptian or Greek equivalent of "bread,"[105] but objects that are peculiar to certain lands or societies are likely to have only one name. The *histōr*, who has been there (whether in a literal, figurative, or rhetorical sense), knows the object as well as its name, which he occasionally offers in a gloss.[106]

A look at the Indian fragments of Ctesias gives us a sense of Herodotus' moderation.[107] The overwhelming majority of exotic animals, plants, foods, weapons, and other artifacts in the *Histories* remain nameless. Glosses that increase strangeness by adding a foreign word are less frequent than familiarizing analogies with objects the audience would recognize. The narrator will

---

[104] See Strauss Clay 1972, esp. 129–131, on *Od.* 10.305 (cf. 12.61) and the similar case at 5.339–342. For the different model of *dinumia* ('double-nameness') in the *Iliad*, see above, p. 33 and note 16.

[105] See above, p. 21 and note 10.

[106] In addition to the glosses discussed in the text in this and in the next sections (2.65.5, 2.69.3, 7.57.3, 9.110.2, 8.98.2, 1.192.2 and 3.89.1, 8.85.3, 2.143.3), see 1.105.4 ("those [affected by the female disease] *whom the Scythians call enareis,*" rendered with *androgunoi* at 4.67.2); 2.77.4 (Egyptians "eat a bread made of barley *which they call kyllestis*"; also in Hecataeus *FrGrHist* 1 F 322); 2.81.1 (Egyptians "wear tunics made of linen with tassels around the ankles *which they call kalasiris*"); 2.92.2 ("water lilies *the Egyptians call lotus*"); 2.94.1 ("the inhabitants of the marshes use an oil from the fruit of the castor, *which the Egyptians call kiki*"); 3.12.4 ("they wear caps *[called] tiaras,*" a loan-word); 4.23. 3 (the Bald Men live off a "*tree called pontikon* . . . the juice of the fruit *is called askhu*"); 4.53.3 (in the Borysthenes there are "*invertebrate fish called antakaioi*"; according to Chamberlain 1999 note 29 this is another transparent word, related to the Greek *anakantha* [ἀνάκανθα] 'invertebrate' given in the text); 5.16.4 (in Lake Prasias in Thrace "there are *two species of fish which they call paprax and tilōn*"); 9.32.1 (Mardonius' army included "*the Calasiries, as they are called,* who were armed with knives and were the only Egyptian fighting men"; cf. 2.164–168). Among the animals at 4.192 only the name of a species of mice is given in Libyan (4.192.3, *zegeries* [ζεγέριες], probably authentic according to Masson 1968.86 and note 11), and then translated into the Greek word *bounoi* (βουνοί) 'hills', for which see Cardona 1976.22. See also the explanation of the Phoenician *Pataikoi* at 3.37.2, and the gloss at 2.73.1 giving the name of the phoenix (on the Egyptian derivation of this word, see Lloyd 1976.317). Only rarely do foreign words simply appear in an ethnography with no metanarrative mediation. These include the mysterious *hualos* (ὕαλος) of Ethiopian burials (3.24.1,2); the Scythian or Massagetan battle-ax, *sagaris* (σάγαρις 1.215.1, 4.5.2, 70, cf. 7.64.2); the Egyptian boat *baris* (βᾶρις 2.41.4 and 5; 2.60.1 and 2, 2.179); and the (in this case Scythian) sword *akinakēs* (ἀκινάκης 4.62). *Baris* is eventually glossed at 2.96.5 and *akinakēs* at 7.54.3 (as a Persian word): see below, pp. 54, 59–60. Some of the unglossed words of Egyptian derivation in Herodotus (see the list by McGready 1968) had probably become a part of Greek vocabulary, e.g. *litron* (λίτρον 2.86, 2.87).

[107] Campos Daroca 1992.150–151. We do not know to what extent and in what way foreign words appearing in other ethnographic writers were mediated by glosses. See e.g. Hecataeus *FGrHist* 1 F 284 (*kupassis,* a Persian dress) and Ctesias *FGrHist* 688 F41 (*sarapis,* Persian trousers).

say, for example: "they have a legume in a pod of the size of a millet seed . . . ."
He mentions no special word for the thing so described.[108]

In some instances, Herodotus provides the foreign term in order to restore the dignity of native names and things in the face of Greek carelessness and contempt. When he discusses the barges which the Egyptians use on the Nile, he starts with the generalized Greek word for boats (*ploia*); he then goes on to explain how they are built flat and with no sides, with boards of acacia wood and papyrus, and how they are pulled upstream from the shore and sail downstream drawn by a raft; finally, he mentions the proper Egyptian term *baris* and draws attention to it ("for this is the name of these boats" 2.96.5). The question of the name does not come up, for example, for the collapsible leather boats of Assyrians, although they are also described at length and given extraordinary importance (1.194). But in the case of the *baris*, we know that Herodotus' fifth-century audience knew the word, if not details about the boat it denoted. In tragedy *baris* is simply a barbarian ship, not specifically for cargo transport on the river, and not even always Egyptian. The brutal Egyptian herald in the *Suppliants* keeps ordering the women onto the *baris*. In the *Persians*, the Elders lament:

Ξέρξης μὲν ἄγαγεν ποποῖ
Ξέρξης δ' ἀπώλεσεν, τοτοῖ
Ξέρξης δὲ πάντα ἐπέσπε δυσφρόνως
βαρίδεσσι ποντίαις.

Xerxes led, woe! Xerxes brought ruin, woe! Xerxes pursued all things insanely with his sea-faring barques.[109]

By describing and naming the Egyptian boat, Herodotus, once again, corrects the Greeks and refines their approximate and ethnocentric knowledge of foreign things, which comes out in a misuse of language.

An inverse display of Greek linguistic ethnocentrism noted by the narrator has to do with crocodiles. In this case the Greeks are at least imprecisely familiar with the exotic thing, but call it by the wrong name. In Egypt crocodiles are not a merely a picturesque feature of the landscape. Herodotus

---

[108] 3.100. See especially the string of comparisons at 2.92.2–4 (five in eight lines). On these comparisons, see especially the discussions by Hartog 1988.225–337, Corcella 1984.68–93, Munson 2001.80–90. That the number of foreign words in Herodotus is relatively small has been noted by Linforth 1926.11; Harrison 1998, ch. 1, "Herodotus' knowledge of foreign languages." The combination of foreign naming and descriptive comparisons appears in Ctesias *FGrHist* 688 F 45.

[109] *Persians* 550–553; cf. 1075. *Suppliants* 836, 873, 882; Broadhead 1960.147; Bacon 1961.15, 20; E. Hall 1989.78. See also Euripides *Iphigeneia at Aulis* 297. Froidefond 1971.96.

gives all sorts of zoological information on these beasts—defamiliarizing through description, one might say in this case—and he especially emphasizes their size and awesome nature. In Egypt, depending on the region, crocodiles are either considered sacred and worshipped or loathed and treated like enemies. At the end of this passage Herodotus provides the Egyptian name with a correction that reveals why he objects to the Greek term:

> However they are not called "crocodiles," but _khampsai_. It was the Ionians who named them "lizards" (κροκόδειλοι) likening their appearance to the lizards which in their country are found in stonewalls.
>
> 2.69.3

The Ionian word _krokodeilos_, in the sense of "crocodile" rather than "lizard," occurs in the _Histories_ for the first time but is by now evidently a part of the Greek language as the only lexical option for denoting these animals.[110] The narrator has been relying on it all along and will continue to do so throughout his _logos_. Herodotus' tacit acceptance of convention in this case recalls the programmatic statement where he begrudgingly concedes that he will, after all, use "Europe," "Asia," and "Libya" as the traditional names of the three continents, in spite of the fact that he finds these _epōnumiai_ ('given names') absurd.[111]

The names of the continents represent the unsigned legacy of an inexplicable tradition. In the case of "crocodiles," the namegivers' identity and motivations are more transparent. Ionian Greeks resident in Egypt and people of that sort, both with the intention to diminish the foreign object and out of ignorance of its _phusis_ (which the _histōr_ undertakes to correct: 2.68.1), have "compared big things with little ones" thoughtlessly and without apology.[112]

---

[110] Unfortunately we cannot be sure of R. Ellis' emendation χάμψα in _Suppliants_ 878, in the Danaids' apostrophe of the Egyptian herald, who is trying to herd them into the _baris_ (see preceding note). Murray 1955 app. Cf. Bacon 1961.21; Friis Johansen, and Whittle 1980 III.209.

[111] 4.45.5. See above, pp. 39, 43. For the term _epōnumia_, see note 24 on page 11.

[112] The narrator of the _Histories_ does this only with great caution: cf. 2.10.1. Lloyd 1976.310 cites other linguistic examples of what he calls the "light-hearted attitude which the Greeks often adopted to things Egyptian": ostriches (_megaloi strouthoi_ [μεγάλοι στρουθοί] 'big sparrows'), obelisks (_obeliskoi_ [ὀβελισκοί] 'little spits'), underground tombs (_saringes_ [σάριγγες] 'pipes'), and pyramids (_puramides_ [πυραμίδες] 'wheatcakes'). Froidefond 1971.122–123 attributes these dismissive names to the defensive snobbery of Greek residents in Egypt, while the Ionian researchers tended to magnify Egyptian things. Herodotus replaces the normal Greek term _katarraktēs_ (καταρράκτης) with the more dramatic _katadoupoi_ (κατάδουποι) and does not use _obeliskos_, but _obelos_. Froidefond 1971.123. Greek re-naming in Egypt is also exemplified by the

The result is a clear case where Greek does not possess the correct verbal imitation of the *pragma* ('thing'), but only a misrepresentation. The *histōr* offers the Egyptian term *champsa*, with additional defamiliarizing effect, as the right name.[113] This passage exemplifies the polemic stance Herodotus assumes against the simplified knowledge the Greeks have constructed to deal with the overwhelming strangeness and magnitude of Egypt (see e.g. 2.15.1). In another context, according to his more usual procedure of making things easier for his audience to apprehend, he is quite willing to say that Libyan crocodiles, of a smaller species, are very similar to lizards.[114]

Orientalism and anti-orientalism

While ethnographic *logoi* provide terms for animals, plants, and artifacts in a variety of barbarian languages, foreign words occur in the historical narrative predominantly in reference to Persian weapons, articles of clothing, and social or political institutions.[115] Herodotus' normal practice is to name foreign institutions in Greek, no matter how different they are from anything for which the Greeks have a specific name. The Persian term *satrapeiē* is offered in a gloss only when a region is first mentioned in the *Histories* as a fiscal unit of the Persian empire (1.192.2), and then once more at the beginning of the description of Darius' reorganization of the provinces (3.89.1). Just as Herodotus' *logos* will travel through "cities" (1.5.3), or Thracian tribesmen are "citizens," so a Persian satrapy is regularly denoted with the term *nomos* ('district') or the more politically charged *arkhē* ('rule').[116] Herodotus' unifying

---

islands Chios, Lesbos, Samos, etc. on the Nile mentioned by Hecataeus (*FGrHist* 1 F 310). Another case when the Greek name of a small animal has been assigned to a different foreign animal seems to be the Indian giant "ants" (*murmēkes* [μύρμηκες]) of 3.102.2. Corcella 1985.69.

[113] A somewhat similar manifestation of ethnocentrism as reflected in language is displayed by the Ethiopian king when he calls bread *kopron* (κόπρον 3.22.4). But as the heirs of a Greek idealizing tradition about people on the margins, the Ethiopians can legitimately laugh at the practices of mainstream cultures. Romm 1992.54–60, esp. 59.

[114] 4.192.2: τῇσι σαυρῇσι ἐμφερέστατοι.

[115] The names of Egyptian castes are given in Greek, with the notice that these groups "take their *ounomata* from their occupations" (2.164.1), though we are also told that "the warriors are called Calasiries and Ermotybies" (2.164.2, cf. 9.39.1).

[116] The term *nomos* (always used of a foreign land) causes ambiguity, e.g. at 9.116.1, where it designates only the Hellespontine area of Thrace, a Persian territorial subdivision smaller than a satrapy. See Asheri 1988b.157. Both terms *arkhē* and *nomos* are also used to denote Egyptian or even Scythian territories. See Powell 1938 *ad voces*. The governor of a Persian province is called *huparkhos* (ὕπαρχος) or *arkhōn* (ἄρχων), the Persian loan-word *satrapēs* (σατράπης) first appearing in Xenophon (Asheri 1988a.378). For the term *poliētai* (πολιῆται 'citizens'), see 5.7, 16.2.

strategy is ideologically significant. By minimizing the linguistic discrepancy between barbarians and Greeks, he encourages the analogy between their respective historical destinies.

A peculiar Persian institution plays an important role in the *Histories*: the system of rewards for meritorious individuals. In the story of the self-mutilation of Zopyrus an ethnographic gloss states that "among the Persians benefactions advance a man to greatness" (3.154.1).[117] The Samian Syloson, who had the good luck to give his cloak to an obscure royal guard named Darius, was appointed tyrant of Samos after the latter became king. Coes, Histiaeus, Mascames, Boges, and Xenagoras received similar honors in exchange for their services.[118] In the Greek world a person may enjoy the status of benefactor vis-à-vis a city, just as it is the city that awards the *aristeia* for valor on the battlefield.[119] At Sparta, the *agathoergoi* ('benefactors') are, in Herodotus' definition, a board of five citizens who for one year "are sent here and there to do errands for the state" (κοινόν, 1.67.5). In Persia, however, what the Greeks call *agathoergiē* (or *euergesiē*) is good service directed to the person of the king. For all the honors it entails, here the status of benefactor marks the individual not as a free citizen but as a subject.[120]

The Persian name of this institution appears once in the *Histories*, in connection with two Ionians from Samos who distinguished themselves for bravery at Salamis. These men deserve special mention, says the narrator, because one of them was later rewarded with the tyranny of Samos and the other was inscribed (ἀνεγράφη) in a special list of benefactors and given a large territory. The status of benefactor is, in other words, an official position: "In Persian (Περσιστί) the benefactors of the king are called *orosangai*" (8.85.3). Herodotus' gloss underlines the cultural anomaly of a Greek who becomes part of the Great King's highest-level retainers for fighting on his behalf against other Greeks in the most important battle of the Persian Wars.

[117] An ethnographic gloss is the explanation of a local custom, in the present tense, inserted in a narrative of past events. Munson 2001.39–40.

[118] 3.139–140, 149, cf. 6.25. 4.97; 5.1; cf. 6.30.2. 7.106–107. 9.107.3. Cf. 7.39.2, 9.18.3 and Thucydides 1.128.4 and 129.3.

[119] E.g. 8.136 (Alexander of Macedon) and 8.11.2. See also the ceremony of awarding honors to citizens who have deserved well of the state at the Great Dionysia in Athens discussed by Goldhill 1990.104–105.

[120] The historical role of the institution of the *orosangai* in securing the Achemaenids' hold on the Persian aristocracy and strengthening their monarchical rule is explored by Briant 1988.97–100. Gould 1991.17–18 (references in his note 51) discusses the institution in the larger context of Herodotus' representation of gift reciprocity. Gift-giving among the Persians and between Persians and Greeks is discussed by Mitchell 1997.111–133, though from later evidence.

In the ethnographical sections, glosses introducing foreign terms constitute an integral part of Herodotus' objective, non-narrated, narrative in the present tense concerning foreign cultures and phenomena.[121] A statement giving the name of a certain type of boat not to be found in Greece is on a continuum with the description of what that boat looks like. In the course of the historical narrative, on the other hand, the appearance of foreign words, whether unmarked or mediated by a gloss, is more conspicuous and likely to raise the issue of orientalism. This term was first employed by Edward Saïd to denote western stereotyped representations of an Eastern setting, which suggest that certain exotic peculiarities go hand in hand with moral shortcomings as the prerogatives of a different world.[122] The application of the concept to ancient Greek texts (not discussed by Saïd) has sometimes lacked subtlety but is nevertheless apt, even in cases when the overall message is not—or not predominantly—derogatory to non-Greeks. In interpreting Aeschylus' *Persians*, to take the most notable example, scholars hold a range of different views: while to some the play comes close to representing a "big racist myth," others see it as a striking demonstration of "the Athenians' ability to explore the suffering of war thorough the eyes of their greatest enemy."[123] No matter what position we take between these two extremes, however, few would deny the presence in the *Persians* of orientalistic elements. These counterbalance the universality of the law of divine retribution for *hubris* by reminding the audience that in this paradigmatic case, at any rate, both the *hubris* and its retribution happened to "them" and not to "us."

The foreignness of Xerxes' invading army in the *Persians* is partly rendered linguistically, through lists of barbarian-sounding proper names.[124] In Herodotus, the catalogue of the same force bristles with "native" (ἐπιχώριον) clothing and equipment, sometimes denoted with foreign or loan words. The

---

[121] A narrative is "non-narrated" or, to be more accurate, minimally narrated when it approaches the pure recording of facts and we least feel the presence of the narrator as a more or less overt mediator between the world of the narrated and the recipient of the narrative. See Chatman 1978.146–266; Genette 1980.212–262.

[122] Saïd 1978.5–9 and passim.

[123] The last quotation is from Dué 2005. I am borrowing "big racist myth" from John Marincola (who used the expression ironically in conversation to characterize an extreme position to which he does not subscribe). In the last fifteen years scholars have tended to emphasize anti-Persian elements in the play (see especially E. Hall 1989.70–72, 76–79; E. Hall 1996; Georges 1994). Others argue for a more complex message where Aeschylus represents the defeated Persians as "other," while at the same time encouraging his Athenian audience to identify with them. See especially the discussion by Dué 2005; Loraux 2002.42–53.

[124] Above, pp. 2–3 and note 12.

Caspians are armed with *akinakai*;[125] Arabs and Thracians wear *zeirai*, apparently a sort of cloak (7.69.1, 7.75.1). The Sacae, a Scythian population, have *kurbasiai* (pointed turbans) and "battle axes *(called) sagaris.*"[126] The Persians use "floppy caps called *tiaras*," *anaxurides* (trousers) and wicker *gerra* "instead of shields."[127] The last item is an important index of the inferiority of Persian light armor at Plataea and Mycale.[128] Persian *anaxurides*, made of leather, connote primitivity to the Lydian Sandanis, but by the time of the Ionian revolt they seem to represent Eastern luxury. Aristagoras mentions them in conjunction not with *tiaras*, but with *kurbasiai* as a sign of inefficiency on the battlefield.[129]

Herodotus' catalogue of Xerxes' force stands midway between ethnography and history, emphasizing internal ethnic diversity as much as overall otherness with respect to the Greeks.[130] In other parts of the narrative of the expedition against Greece, however, the orientalistic tradition of the Greek representation of the Persians is unmistakable. When he feels so inclined, Xerxes rides in a *harmamaxa*, a light covered chariot, which is also used to transport the gold-decked concubines and the retinue of the Persian commanders. This piece of furnishing is ridiculed in Aristophanes' *Acharnians*; it almost certainly represents the "wheeled tent" mentioned in the *Persians*.[131] In the context of the conflict between Greece and Persia, Herodotus uses the term *barbaros* more frequently than in the earlier books;[132] he reports two oracles that call the Persians *barbarophōnoi* (8.20.2; 9.43.3); and he uniquely qualifies, in his own voice, the flogging of the Hellespont as *barbaros* in the sense of "barbaric" (7.35.2). A follow-up of that scene contains another orientalistic use of a Persian word. Perhaps regretting his previous desecration, Xerxes throws into the Hellespont precious offerings, including "a Persian

---

[125] 7.67.1; the sword is not named but described as part of the equipment of the Persian contingent (7.61, and cf. Pollux I 138; cited by Legrand 1951.91). In an ethnographic context it also appears as a Scythian sword (4.62.2, 3; 4.70). For the use of the word as a Persian sword at 7.54.2 and other narrative passages, see below and note 133.

[126] 7.64.2. Also mentioned in the Massagetan and Scythian ethnographies: 1.215.1, 4.5.3, 4.70.

[127] 7.61.1. Wearing of tiaras make Persian skulls soft (3.12); a tiara is worn by the sacrificer in the Persian ethnography (1.132.1); made of gold, it is a royal gift (8.120). Cf. *Persians* 661. On the Persian "Median" or "rider custom," see Miller 1997.156–157.

[128] 9.61.3, 62.2, 99.3, 102.2 and 3. See Flower and Marincola 2002.214, with figure on frontispiece.

[129] 1.71.2 (cf. 3.87, the trousers of Darius' groom); 5.59.3. To the Greeks, "*anaxurides* emblematized all that was foreign about Iranians" (Miller 1997.185).

[130] On the character of the Herodotus' catalogue, see Payen 1997.102–103.

[131] ἁρμάμαξα: 7.41, 83.2, 9.76.1; cf. *Acharnians* 69–70; Aeschylus *Persians* 1000–1001. Miller 1997.62.

[132] Levy 1991.195 and note 11 counts 24 instances of the stem *barbar-* up to 5.23, and 179 in the rest of the work.

sword *they call <u>akinakes</u>"* (7.54.2). Elsewhere in the *Histories*, Persian *akinakai* are precious gifts for the friends of the king or booty for the victorious Greeks. They are used to dispatch a dishonest satrap and cut off the ears and noses of royal guards.[133]

Herodotus' dialogism provides, to be sure, compensatory elements. When the Persian army arrives to Achaean Halos in Thessaly, he reports at some length the local story (ἐπιχώριον λόγον) of Athamas' murder of Phrixus with the pretext that the guides told it to Xerxes "wishing to inform him of everything" (7.197.1). As a consequence of Athamas' crime, they say, the Achaeans sacrifice the oldest sons of the family that descend from Phrixus if they disobey the prohibition from entering their *lēiton* ('people's hall'), the term by which "the Achaeans call the *prutanēion* ('town-hall')" (7.197.2). It has been suggested that Herodotus makes Xerxes pass through Halos precisely in order to have the opportunity to make this digression.[134] The almost unheard of case of human sacrifices among the Greeks parallels those made by the Persians during the march.[135] Here Xerxes listens to details of the Achaean ritual, shows his reverence, and moves on. In space and narrative, he has already entered Greece and is approaching Thermopylae. Yet he is still, as Herodotus implies linguistically and otherwise, in a foreign world.

Even if not all that is alien and brutal is also barbarian, however, considerable corruption exists at the Persian king's court. In the last Xerxes narrative in the *Histories*, an ethnographic gloss places adultery, female power, and bloody excess in the context of the *nomos* of a royal feast. This passage contains a translation in two stages, as in some of the glosses to proper names we have already seen.[136] The marked introduction of the foreign word is followed by an etymology that renders its expressiveness back into Greek:

> [Amestris] waits for the day in which her husband Xerxes is due to offer the royal banquet—<u>this banquet is given once a year on the king's birthday; the name of this banquet in Persian (Περσιστί) is</u>

---

[133] 8.120, 9.80.2; 3.118.2; 3.128.5. See also 9.107.2. Cf. above, p. 59 and note 125. On the literary and archaeological evidence for Persian *akinakai*, see Miller 1997.46–48.

[134] Macan 1908.1.192.

[135] 7.114. Human sacrifice is also perhaps recorded for the Persians at 7.180, and see 1.86.2. It is otherwise a custom only in Herodotus' ethnographies about Massagetae (1.216.2), Padaean Indians (3.99), Scythians (4.62, 71–72), Taurians (4.103), and various Thracian tribes (4.94, 5.5, 9.119). It is normally regarded, at any rate, as a quintessentially barbarian practice: Plutarch *On Superstition* 171B–E and Nikolaidis 1986.138. On the Achaean episode in Herodotus 7.197, see Crahay 1954.89–91.

[136] E.g. 4.110.1; see above, pp. 37–38.

tukta and in Greek (κατὰ [τὴν] Ἑλλήνων γλῶσσαν) *telēion* ('perfect'): on that occasion only, the king anoints his head with perfumes and gives presents to the Persians; having waited, then, for this day, Amestris asks Xerxes to be given the wife of Masistes as a present.

9.110.2

Tukta is apparently another transparent word, close to *tuktos* (τυκτός [τευχ-]).[137] Both the Homeric *tuktos* and the classical word *telēios* (τελήιος), which Herodotus gives as a translation for *tukta*, are used to describe either finished and well-made good things or "perfect" evils.[138] The result of this beautiful royal festivity is in fact complete disaster. The king feels bound by custom (*hupo tou nomou*) to comply with the request of his wife because whatever one asks at the royal banquet must be granted (9.111.1). Amestris proceeds to mutilate her rival by cutting off her ears, lips, tongue, and breasts and throwing the last to the dogs. The victim's husband, Masistes (who is also Xerxes' brother), runs off to Bactria with the intention of provoking a revolt against the king, but he and his children are killed en route, so that his house is entirely destroyed (9.111–113).

The *tukta* gloss closely connects the ethnographer's descriptions of customs and the historian's reconstruction of the past. The banquet is a key-event of Persian culture, a feature in some sense symbolic of what the Persians are (or rather, of what they have become after the foundation of the empire by Cyrus), and a means of displaying their civilization vis-à-vis the rest of the world.[139] The occasions and etiquette of Persian dinners, how much and what they eat, what the Persians themselves think of these things, and how the Greeks regard them are recurrent topics both in the Persian ethnography and in the historical narrative.[140] The *tukta* is the *non-plus ultra* of Persian banquets, celebrated on the most solemn of birthdays. It is also an occasion, however, on

[137] Chamberlain 1999.276n29.

[138] See LSJ *ad voces*. Most scholars interpret the terms in the Herodotean passage as referring to the magnificence of the occasion. However Benveniste 1965.485 interprets it as "'acquitté' ou 'acquis'"; Masaracchia 1978.210 considers it a reference to the completion of the year by the king.

[139] For the notion of "key-event," see Fetterman 1989.5. Clifford Geertz's analysis of the Balinese cockfight as revelatory of "what being a Balinese 'is really like'" develops the same concept though he does not use the term (Geertz 1973.412–453, esp.417).

[140] In the Persian ethnography, see the section on birthdays and banquets at 1.133 and cf. the ethnographic gloss at 3.79.3. In the historical narrative banquets mark crucial moments at the beginning of Persian history (1.125–126) and at the end of their imperialistic dream with the defeat of Plataea (9.82). Other instances: 1.207.6–7 with 211, 7.119, 7.135.1. In Thucydides 1.130.1 Pausanias "keeps a Persian table."

which the king appears with his head uncovered and smears it with perfumes; that is to say, he steps down somewhat from his exalted position. He is still the king because he can fulfill all wishes, but he is less than king since he cannot refuse to do so. The ethnographic-linguistic note does more than underline the decadent luxury of the Persians, according to the most elementary level of the stereotype. It cooperates with the historical narrative of this particular banquet to convey the ambiguity between stately protocol and royal capriciousness, between the Persian king's omnipotence and his ultimate lack of control.

For Herodotus, the instability of order and justice in Persian culture derives from the monarchy and its *nomoi*. The ideological opposite of the *tukta* is the Persian postal system, which Herodotus describes in a gloss that leaves the monarchy as much as possible aside. In Aeschylus' *Agamemnon*, the beacon-to-beacon fire that announces the king's return from Troy is qualified by the adjectival form *angaros* (ἄγγαρος), with a sinister reference to the barbarism of the doomed house of Atreus (282). Herodotus gives the noun *angarēion* (ἀγγαρήιον) for the relay of couriers used to convey official communications across the huge distances of the empire. The gloss intervenes between Xerxes' dispatch of news of the disaster of Salamis and their arrival to Susa. In contrast with the popular jubilation at Xerxes' capture of Athens, the narrative describes the mourning in terms that recall the extravagant and womanly lamentations in Aeschylus' *Persians*.[141] Precisely at this humiliating narrative moment for the Persians, the *histōr* reestablishes the representational equilibrium by describing the messenger system. Persian ingenuity, efficiency, endurance, and dedication—all the qualities the Persians did not, could not, display at Salamis—are embodied in this institution, a collective Persian invention (τοῖσι Πέρσῃσι ἐξεύρηται) that suggests a superior counterpart of Greek professional messenger guilds.[142] The run of negative sentences emphasizes a cooperative effort surpassing all standards of excellence:

> No mortal being is swifter than these messengers. This is how this
> system has been devised by the Persians: for they say that according
> to how many days it takes to make the journey, a certain number
> of horses and men is stationed at the interval of one day's journey.

[141] τοὺς κιθῶνας κατερρήξαντο πάντες, βοῇ τε καὶ οἰμωγῇ ἐχρέωντο ἀπλέτῳ (8.99.2); cf. the Chorus' description of the mourning of Persian women in *Persians* 121–134, 531–538, which will be reproduced by the womanly Elders themselves and Xerxes. Georges 1994.92, 102–104. For tearing of robes, see *Persians* 125, 199, 468, 537–538.

[142] E.g. the Athenian and Argive *hēmerodromoi* (6.105.1, 9.12.1) and the *Talthybiadai* of Sparta (7.134.1).

> Neither snow, nor rain, nor heat, nor night holds them back from
> the accomplishment of their duty.
>
> 8.98.1–2

A gloss of comparison makes the foreign phenomenon both familiar and
endearing by assimilating it to a Greek religious and athletic context:

> The one who runs first then passes the message on to the second,
> the second to the third, and so on it passes from the one to the
> other, just as among the Greeks there is the torch-race they run in
> honor of Hephaestus.[143]

Finally, by a metanarrative counter-move, the institution is returned to its
owners and dignified with its proper term: "The Persians call this course of
horse-post *angarēion*" (8.98.2).

Orientalism is woven into the very fabric of the contemporary Greek
representation of barbarians, and Herodotus knows how to exploit it for
didactic aims. But his Persian couriers are remarkably "Western," and, as it
turns out, we have enlisted them twenty-four centuries after the *Histories* to
represent ourselves.[144]

Language and relativity

Herodotus assumes a large sphere of equivalence among different foreign
languages and Greek, yet he goes even further by establishing the autonomous
validity and intelligibility of barbarian speech both within and outside
that sphere. Cultures are entitled to their names, and Greek replacements
are often wrong. One can correctly translate into Greek names that signify

---

[143] On the rhetorical genre of this analogy, see Hartog 1988.226–227.

[144] An excerpt from Herodotus 8.98.2 has been inscribed above the 280-foot frieze of the New York
U.S. General Post Office Building, which opened to the public on Labor Day, September 1914.
(The building has since been named the James A. Farley Building, and will soon be renamed
again and, alas, no longer be mainly a post-office). Mr. William Mitchell Kendall of the firm
McKim, Mead and White, the architects who planned the building, supplied the Herodotean
passage in his own English translation. I am grateful to Mr. Joseph H. Cohen, curator of the New
York Museum of Postal History, for providing me with this information. Though the ideological
bases for Mr. Kendall's choice for the inscription are unknown, the allusion to the tradition of
the Pony Express in the American West seems to me unmistakable, confirming the sense of
self-identification elicited by this passage among North-American readers. The word *angarēion*
has had a more orientalistic development, for which see Asheri and Corcella 2003.98: it came to
denote forced labor in Greek, the Roman *cursus publicus* in Latin (*angaria, angarium*), and *corvée*
(forced labor) or abuse in European languages (e.g., Italian *angheria*).

logoi and evaluate whether they describe reality in an accurate way. Foreign phenomena unknown to the Greeks need to be explained and sometimes given their accurate native name. To translate or explain is neither problematic nor difficult, but it requires the appropriate adjustment of the available Greek terms to the realities of a different world.

A word for word translation may serve to minimize cultural or ideological discrepancies, as in the case of satrapies/*arkhai*.[145] Other times it throws it into sharper relief ('benefactors'/*orosangai*). In a few precious cases, moreover, linguistic heteroglossia is an opportunity for questioning Greek cultural knowledge and breaking away from its constraints. A gloss that intervenes to explain a word in a preceding utterance enhances the sudden sense of discovery of a different and instructive world-view.[146]

On the footsteps of Hecataeus of Miletus, Herodotus discusses matters of chronology with an Egyptian priest, who shows him the colossal wooden statues of many generations of *piromis* priests. The foreign word is focalized through the local guide, but the narrator immediately explains that: "*Piromis* is in Greek *kalos kagathos*" (2.143.3). The equivalence seems simple enough but the proportions are wrong, just as the Egyptian standard of measure (the *schoenus*) is many times in excess of the Persian and Greek measures.[147] The narrative has already qualified the translation of *piromis* in advance by placing side-by-side Hecataeus, a Milesian *kalos kagathos* (i.e., a member of the Greek aristocracy) and the Egyptian *piromis* priest. To the first, who boasted sixteen generations of ancestors leading up to a god, the latter showed physical proof of 345 with no divine figure in sight. Instructed by the experience of Hecataeus and perhaps less genealogically privileged than he, the *histōr* of the *Histories* knows better than to enter a competition with the Egyptian priest: he relates

---

[145] This happens also when a Greek word is given as a foreign name, but with a meaning somewhat different than it normally has in Greek. See 2.171: "They give near this lake representations of his (i.e., Osiris', not named) passion, *which the Egyptians call 'mysteries'*." Here Froidefond 1971.191 maintains that a discrepancy is implicit between the way in which the Egyptians use the linguistic equivalent of the Greek word μυστήρια and the Greek use, as in "Eleusinian Mysteries" (*Contra* Lloyd 1976.279, who regards this as a straightforward case of *interpretatio Graeca* on Herodotus' part). Similarly, the plant "*which the Egyptians call lotus*" (2.92.2, where λωτός is supposed to represent an Egyptian word, not a translation: see Lloyd 1976.171) is different from the Cyrenaic lotus assumed as more familiar to the audience at 2.96, the fruit of which is described at 4.177.

[146] See above, p. 30 and note 3.

[147] The Egyptian *schoenos* "means" (*dunatai*) sixty stades, the *parasang* thirty stades (2.6.3). Herodotus gives the measurements of Egypt in *skhoenoi*, which he says is the standard of the magnate landowner, while the rich man measures his land in *parasangs*, the man of modest property in stades, and the land-poor in fathoms (2.6.1–2).

his predecessor's experience, corroborates the evidence of the *piromis* statues, and translates as best he can, although not without irony, the *piromis* name.[148] Language can only reflect what a society knows, and what the Greeks know is based on the manipulation of a narrow experience, in time as in space.[149]

Foreign cultures also confound Greek subjectivity when they display their own. The Egyptians, who write numbers and letters from right to left (ἀπὸ τῶν δεξιῶν ἐπὶ τὰ ἀριστερά) instead of from left to right, *say* they do things "rightly" (or "to the right": ἐπιδέξια ποιέειν) and the Greeks wrongly (or "to the left": ἐπαρίστερα).[150] They also subdivide political space into Egyptians and everyone else, just as the Greeks have created the antithesis between Greeks and non-Greeks. After reporting an Egyptian prophecy that refers to the Persians as "barbarians," the narrator translates: "The Egyptians call '*barbaroi*' all those who do not speak the same language as themselves" (πάντας ... τοὺς μὴ σφίσι ὁμογλώσσους) (2.158.5). Elsewhere, the text cites the Persians as claiming dominion over the "the barbarian peoples" of Asia (1.4.4); but does the expression come from the narrator or does it reproduce the sources' speech? If the latter is the case, are the Persians referring to the non-Persian nations of Asia or are they adopting their interlocutors' point of view ("We are barbarians and other barbarian nations are our affair")? In the Egyptian passage, the narrator eliminates all ambiguity and deconstructs the Greek fantasy about non-Greeks applying the term *barbaroi* to themselves.[151] His translation of the Egyptian oracle alerts the listener about the existence of some Egyptian word semantically equivalent—and perhaps phonetically similar—to the Greek *barbaros*, but not applicable to the same referent.[152] On

---

[148] Thissen 1993.243.

[149] Froidefond 1971.137–139; Hunter 1982.50–72. For a skeptical view on the historical authenticity of Herodotus' *piromis* episode, see West 1991.145–149.

[150] 2.36.4. Is this a value judgment Herodotus translates with a pun, or is the Egyptian terminology for "right" and "left" the opposite of that of the Greeks? For the first interpretation, see Lloyd 1976.36–37, following Spielberg 1921. The second, suggested by Vasunia 2001.137, causes problems (what did Herodotus think the Egyptian words for "right" and "left" sounded like?), but is also possible.

[151] A pervasive phenomenon in drama and elsewhere: e.g. Aeschylus *Persians* 635; Euripides *Hecuba* 481–482; Xenophon *Anabasis* 1.7.3–4. In Herodotus, aside from 2.158.5 and (perhaps) 1.4.4, the word *barbaros* is only used by Greeks, and always to denote the foreigner in relation to Greeks or Greek-speakers.

[152] According to Lloyd 1988.157–158, the words by which the Egyptians referred to foreigners did not encode the notion of *language* difference; this makes it all the more remarkable that a Greek author would have assumed that to have been the case. Cf. Thissen 1993.243. For foreign words given by Herodotus already translated into Greek, see above, p. 31 and note 8. On the

the Greek side, Spartan idiom confuses *barbaros* (non-Greek) with *xenos* (non-Spartan stranger and guest).[153] Among non-Greeks, the Egyptians call *barbaroi*, or 'noise-makers', all non-Egyptians, including the Greeks.[154]

As we have already mentioned, Plato's theoretical statements about the equal validity of Greek and non-Greek languages in the *Cratylus* seem connected to his rejection elsewhere of the whole Greek-barbarian antithesis: the non-Athenian character named *Xenos* in the *Statesman* argues in fact that this subdivision is based entirely on the existence of the word *barbaros*, and not on anything objective or real.[155] In a more empirical way, simply by translating words, Herodotus makes comparable points: barbarian speech shows both that the notion of the linguistic handicap of non-Greeks is invalid and that the barbarian/non-barbarian antithesis is relative. Like the name of the continents and "crocodile," so the conventional term *barbaros* is not "correct." It does not convey an appropriate representation of its object, in whatever language.

national languages used by oracles and on the *histōr*'s competence to understand them, see below, pp. 78–83.

[153] 9.11.3. See above, pp. 16–18.

[154] That this episode in Herodotus undermines the Greek-barbarian antithesis was already noticed by Baldry 1965.21. Braund 1998.178.

[155] 262c10–263a. Baxter 1992. See above, p. 45. Braund 1998.178n29.

4

THE MEANING OF LANGUAGE DIFFERENCE

On misunderstanding language difference

IN RELATION TO THE STANDARDS against which he measures himself, the *histōr* of the *Histories* possesses a multi-lingual competence that contrasts with the sense of strangeness most Greek-speakers experience when confronted with any barbarian speech. In his narrative of the common origins of the oracles of Zeus-Ammon in Libya and of Zeus at Dodona,[1] Herodotus communicates his own understanding of the linguistic aspect of the psychology of otherness. According to the Egyptian priests of Zeus at Thebes, Phoenicians once abducted two priestesses from their temple and separately sold them into slavery, one in Libya and the other in northern Greece, where they each founded a sanctuary (2.54). The priestesses at Dodona, however, told the *histōr* a different story, also supported by "the other Dodonians from around the sanctuary." According to this version, two black doves flew from Egyptian Thebes, one to Libya and the other to Greece. The dove that arrived in Greece, the Dodonians say, perched on top of an oak tree at Dodona, and spoke out "with human voice" (φωνῇ ἀνθρωπείη). It declared that a sanctuary of Zeus must rise on that spot. The local people assumed that this was an announcement from god (θεῖον) and obeyed. Meanwhile, the other dove established the sanctuary of Ammon in Libya (2.55).

Confronted with these two traditions, Herodotus offers his own interpretation (γνώμη), which is far more than an attempt to reconcile them and establish what really happened. In speculating on how the more fantastic Dodonian legend may have originated, the narrator reflects on the process of naming and the transmission of names. Since the Egyptian version seems at least

---

[1] Cf. 2.42.5: "The Egyptians call Zeus 'Ammon'." For the tradition of the common origin of Siwa and Dodona and the controversy about the origins of the two stories reported by Herodotus, see Lloyd 1976.253–254; Fehling 1989.65–70; Nesselrath 1999.

plausible from a rationalist viewpoint, Herodotus starts by assuming as true (εἰ ἀληθέως) the story of the Phoenician abduction that caused the arrival of two priestesses (not doves), one to Libya and the other to Greece, or—as it was then called—Pelasgia.[2] The woman who came to Dodona, he says, must have built a shrine of Zeus under the oak tree in remembrance of the sanctuary she used to tend at home. After learning Greek (συνέλαβε τὴν Ἑλλάδα γλῶσσαν), she founded an oracle and told the local people about how her sister was sold in Libya by the same men who sold her in Thesprotia. Where, then, did the Greek tradition about doves come from? This is how Herodotus explains it:

> It seems to me that the reason why these women were called "doves" by the Dodonians is this, that they were *barbaroi*, and seemed to them to speak like birds. After a while they say she started to speak with human voice (ἀνθρωπείη φωνῇ), when the woman uttered sounds that were intelligible to them (συνετά σφι ηὔδα). So long as the woman was speaking barbarian (ἐβαρβάριζε), she seemed to them to be speaking with the voice of birds—for could a dove really speak with human voice? And when they say that the dove was black, they indicate (σημαίνουσι) that the woman was Egyptian.

2.57

Black, foreign, and a slave, the woman has been confined to the animal world, yet at the same time regarded as the bearer of a divine message. To the ancient Pelasgians of Dodona, "human voice" is the Greek language and barbarian speech is abnormal in either direction.[3] But how could anyone fathom a speaking dove? To the Pelasgians, no doubt, the Egyptian priestess is a "dove" in somewhat the same way as to the Scythians snow is "feathers" or to the narrator himself certain Ethiopians sound like bats. The process of transmission, however, has turned the woman into a literal dove just as—less innocently—Cyrus' nurse Spako became a dog in the discourse of political propaganda. In the case of the Dog-woman the motivation of the initial name-givers is unimportant and unclear, but for the Dove-woman it is crucial and solves the riddle. When the present-day Dodonians say "black dove," they

---

[2] On Herodotus' rationalization on the basis of the likely, see Lloyd 1976.252, Campos Daroca 1992.57.

[3] The Greek assimilation of barbarian language to the voice of birds (see above, p. 3 and note 15) coexists with the older tradition according to which the voice of birds is also a metaphor for the voice of the poet (see e.g. Alcman PMG 39, 40) who produces speech that is abnormal but close to that of the gods. See Nagy 1990.88. Here skin color is predictably a secondary index of otherness. Snowden 1983.

unwittingly give a sign (*sēmainousi*) of the truth to Herodotus, who speaks their same "language," but is also aware of many different languages and knows that common to all of them is the mythopoetic power of names.[4]

Linguistic ethnocentrism entails a claim to the privileged and absolute status of utterances: for the Greeks, only Greek has meaning and what has meaning is Greek. This attitude is mortified in the episode of the defeat of the Greeks from Perinthus at the hands of a barbarian tribe, the Thracian Paeonians (5.1.2–3). One would like to call this little story an *ainos*, a coded narrative designed to teach a general point.[5] Here Paeonians and Perinthians, to paraphrase one of Plutarch's complaints about Herodotus, seem to play the role of crows and monkeys in the fables of Aesop.[6]

We have seen cases in the *Histories* when Herodotus discovers word-transparency as a sort of secret weapon for decoding barbarian speech. Other times, however, he does just the opposite, and criticizes those who understand foreign words in terms of Greek.[7] The Paeonian-Perinthian narrative belongs to this second category of passages, since it features a single sound, *Paion*, which means different things to different peoples. For the Greeks this is a name of Apollo the Savior and of a song in which Apollo is invoked in this way.[8] For the Paeonians, on the other hand, *Paion* means 'Paeonian', and is the name by which they call themselves. Both *ethnea* in the story appear oblivious to this distinction or, for that matter, to the existence of any language beside their own.

Unlike the *logos* of the doves, this one is sparingly narrated, with no metanarrative interventions. Its mildly anti-Greek bias derives from its being

---

[4] Spako: 1.110.1. Scythian "feathers": 4.31. Ethiopians speaking like bats: 4.183.4. Cf. Mora 1985.191. See above, pp. 40–41 and 25.

[5] In Greek *ainos* may refer to any allusive utterance; in Nagy's definition, it represents "a code that carries the right message for those who are qualified and the wrong message or messages for those who are unqualified" (Nagy 1990.148). Herodotus never uses the term, but the *epea* or *logoi* uttered by some of his characters bear a secondary meaning that makes them substantially equivalent to *ainoi*: see, for example, the story about the flute player and the fish that Cyrus tells the Ionians (1.141.1), and the other cases discussed by Hollmann 1998.116–125. Moreover, as Nagy has argued, the Herodotus narrator himself, though he employs the medium of *historiē*, also participates in the mode of the *ainos* vis-à-vis his audiences. Nagy 1990.215–338. Also Payen 1997.66–74; Munson 2001.5–8.

[6] *Malice of Herodotus* 40 = *Moralia* 871D: "Thus Herodotus no longer picks Scythians or Persians or Egyptians to utter the sayings which he invents himself—as Aesop picks crows and apes . . ." (trans. L. Pearson). Nagy 1990.322 quotes this passage in his discussion of the generic connections between Herodotus and Aesop.

[7] See above, p. 12 and note 28; pp. 35, 44, 48–49.

[8] See e.g. *Homeric Hymn III to Apollo* 500, 517–519.

focalized through the Paeonians and from the outcome of the action, which is comically detrimental to the Perinthians. The Paeonians had received an oracle from "the god," encouraging them to make war on the Perinthians. When the two armies would be ranked opposite to each other, the oracle had said, if the Paeonians should hear the Perinthians call their name, they should immediately attack and victory would be theirs. Subsequently, Perinthians and Paeonians got together for a series of contests. The Perinthians won and began to sing the paean. The Paeonians thought that the Perinthians were calling their name and that their moment had come, just as the oracle had said. They promptly attacked the Perinthians and inflicted on them a severe defeat.

In Aeschylus' *Persians*, the paean is followed by a perfectly articulate war-song on freedom; it serves as a glorious affirmation of Greek superiority vis-à-vis the confused "clamor of tongue," γλώσσης ῥόθος, of the barbarians before the battle.[9] In the *Persians* by Timotheus, the paean will celebrate the victory (210–214) and contrast with the ungrammatical supplication of a Persian prisoner "entwining Greek with his Asiatic tongue."[10] The Greeks do not sing the paean in the more complicated Herodotean narrative of Salamis.[11] That song appears in the Paeonian episode instead, where it works as an instrument of defeat for those who sing it and an incitement to victory for those who have misunderstood its intended meaning. "The god," not identified by name and culturally neutral, has this time for reasons unknown favored the barbarians, denying the privilege of meaning to Greek and presiding over the equal status of languages.

Language makes no difference

If linguistic relativity is the main point of the Perinthian-Paeonian narrative, the aim of conveying that message helps to explain the uniqueness of the story in other respects. It is somewhat obscure, mock-heroic in tone, and it represent the situation, unusual in the *Histories*, of an oracle that encourages someone to go to war and practically rewards aggression.[12] This is also the only case in

[9] *Persians* 393, 406. Hall 1996.139. See also 605, where a κέλαδος οὐ παιώνιος (i.e., a cry antithetical to a *paion*, because barbarian) rings in the queen's ears. Discussed by Broadhead 1960.159–160.

[10] Timotheus *Persians* 158–159: Ἑλλάδ' ἐμπλέκων Ἀσιάδι φωνάν. I am quoting the text as edited by Wilamowitz-Moellendorf, reprinted by Janssen 1984.

[11] A barbarian scream in a battle context appears in the oracle reported at 9.43.3. For the ambivalence of Herodotus' representation of the battle of Salamis, see Munson 1988; 2001.223–224.

[12] For Herodotus' attitude toward wars of aggression, see Munson 2001.211–217.

Herodotus when misunderstanding the national verbal code causes trouble or otherwise affects the course of events.[13] Elsewhere in the *Histories*, only once does someone strategically exploit language difference against an enemy in war: this is Leotychides in his message to the Ionians on the eve of Mycale, a maneuver that however remains without clear results.[14] Conversely, speaking the same national language is not a cure-all. The only Greek in the *Histories* who knows a foreign language, the Persian-speaking Histiaeus, ends up impaled by his Persian captors anyway.[15] The Greeks are *homoglōssoi*, yet they do not talk to each other; instead, they solve their differences by war (7.9.β1–2).

In Herodotus, as in Homer and tragedy, speakers of different tongues engage in mutual dialogue without technical difficulties.[16] When an anonymous Persian shares with Greek symposiasts Greek-like sentiments concerning the imminent battle of Plataea, we exceptionally learn that he uses the Greek language (Ἑλλάδα γλῶσσαν ἱέντα).[17] In other narratives the only issue is implicitly whether or not barbarian characters "speak Greek" in a figurative sense, expressing conceptually what a Greek would express,[18] or whether their utterances are distinctly alien. Cultural misunderstandings occur and, like the misinterpretation of oracles, may have a linguistic component.[19] The failure of communication between Croesus and Solon, for example, involves the two speakers' different notions of who should "be called" *olbios* and of the

[13] Cf. e.g. Polybius 1.67.9 on the difficulties of communication in the Carthaginian army (cited by Rotolo 1972.405).

[14] 9.98.2. No such attempt appears in the parallel message of Themistocles (8.22.2). Cases of strategic exploitation of language difference in other sources include Thucydides 3.112, Aeschylus *Libation Bearers* 563–564, Liv. 1.27.9; cited by Rotolo 1972.402 and note 35.

[15] 6.29.2. Foreign-speaking Greeks are remarkably rare also in other text, but see, e.g. Themistocles, who devoted a year studying Persian before presenting himself to the Great King (Thucydides 1.138.1, and see Gehman 1914.35 for other sources on this story).

[16] For the convention, see Lejeune 1940–1948.51. E. Hall 1989.117–121.

[17] 9.16.2. The specification agrees with the extreme precision of the source citation in this case.

[18] See the words by which Croesus exonerates Adrastus (1.45.2) or Idanthyrsus challenges Darius (4.127.1–4). The introduction to the Constitutional Debate (3.80.1) communicates the narrator's deliberate program to demonstrate to his audience that intellectual insights, moral principles, and values which contemporary ideology regarded as typically Greek are actually not the exclusive prerogative of Greeks. In Aeschylus' *Persians* a barbarian has to be a ghost and, as Georges put it, "laundered" and universalized by death before he can speak with the moral consciousness of a Greek (Georges 1994.82, cf. 110.).

[19] See e.g. the Persian difficulties in translating the non-verbal Scythian message of Darius. For oracles, cf. Heraclitus DK 93: "the god neither discloses nor hides his thought but indicates through signs (σημαίνει)." Hence the difficulty normally consists in recognizing a metaphor as such and decoding its correct referent (e.g. 1.55). Kirchberg 1965; Bernabò 1977. For this and other meanings of the verb σημαίνειν in Herodotus, see Hollmann 1998.10–16.

meaning of that term.[20] But no consequence ever results in the *Histories* from Greek-speakers, Lydian-speakers, Persian-speakers, etc., not understanding one another because of their national languages.

The role of language difference in the sphere of communication and mutual acceptance clearly emerges from those narratives that explicitly raise the issue. When a group of reckless young Nasamones from influential families went to explore the deserts of Libya and was captured by pygmies, "neither did the Nasamones know a word of their language, nor did those who took them away know the language of the Nasamones" (2.32.6). This negation signals impending trouble, but the text does not deliver on its apparent promise: the Nasamones returned home safe and sound (2.33.1). Again in Libya, Herodotus describes a system of commercial bargaining between Carthaginians and a local tribe that must rely on dumb show and smoke signals (4.196). These transactions work quite well, and "there is no foul play on either side" (ἀδικέειν δὲ οὐδετέρους, 4.196.3). The negative evaluation here represents an implicit response to the expectation of the listener.[21]

The topic of speech forms a counterpoint to the main plot of an ethno-graphic-historical narrative—another *ainos*—designed to undermine conventional notions of alterity:[22] the story of the gradual coming together and ultimate fusion of a band of Scythian young men and a parallel contingent of stranded Amazons or, as the Scythians call them, "Mankillers."[23] The two groups are in principle as mutually incompatible as Amazons and Greeks—or as Greeks and barbarians, the antithesis they symbolize. In practice, however they turn out to be equal and remarkably similar, except in gender and language. As one of the Amazons and the young Scythian who approaches her start dealing with one another in their primitive setting, the narrative again specifies that the two were not able to communicate through speech, but that it was not a problem:

> [the Amazon] was not able to speak with her voice (φωνῆσαι) since they did not understand one another, but she told him with her hand (χειρὶ ἔφραζε) to come the next day to the same place and

---

[20] 1.29–34.1. The ambiguity of the concept of *olbos* etc. is discussed by Nagy 1990.274–282. For Croesus as the symbol of man bombarded with verbal communications he is unable to interpret, see Sebeok and Brady 1979.

[21] For the role of negation in the ethnographies, see Munson 2001.148.

[22] For *ainos*, see above, p. 69 and note 5.

[23] 4.110–117. The gloss with the Scythian name *Oiorpata* has been quoted above, p. 38. On this episode, see, especially Dewald 1981, Hartog 1988.217–224, Flory 1987.108–113, Munson 2001a.123–132. Also Campos Daroca 1992.45, 47.

bring another man with him, making a sign (σημαίνουσα) that there should be two, and that she would bring another woman with her.

4.113.2

Just as sex replaces war, here the universal language of gestures overcomes the language barrier.[24] This first encounter leads to others, and at the end of the story they all get married, Scythians and Amazons, and the Sauromatian nation is born. The text brings up again the issue of language as part of the well-balanced distribution of powers and privileges between the two equal groups in the new society. The Amazons adopt the language of their Scythian husbands. This corresponds to their subordinate position in the sexual sphere but it is also, in Herodotus' formulation, an index of superior intelligence: "the men were not able to learn (οὐκ ἐδυνέατο μαθεῖν) the language of the women, but the women picked up the language of the men" (4.114.1). Nevertheless, "the Amazons did not learn it perfectly"; as a result the Sauromatae basically speak Scythian, but they distort it (σολοικίζοντες, 4.117). While Herodotus employs the verb *soloikizein* 'distort' in this remark on a dialect which is not, alas, pure Scythian, in other texts the word is applied to bad *Greek* as a virtual synonym of *barbarizein*.[25] But by cheerfully assuming the Scythian viewpoint, the ethnographer once again scores a point for relativity on the language front.

The narrative of the *Histories* occasionally indicates the existence of a linguistic discrepancy between speakers simply by recording that someone was in charge of mediating a verbal exchange. Interpreters must have been a regular feature of international transactions in the ancient world. Xenophon mentions them rather frequently, sometimes by name, and occasionally gives them a minor character role.[26] In Herodotus' narrative, which follows tragic and poetic conventions, interpreters are an optional feature and appear only four times, always as part of the apparatus of the Persian court.[27] Their role, however, is different from that of guards, gatekeepers, and other enforcers of the king's power.[28] Just as in glosses of *historiē* interpreters occasionally facili-

[24] For gestures that cross cultural boundaries, see above, p. 22.

[25] The word occurs only here in Herodotus and is not attested earlier. But *L.S.* s.v. cite the definition τῇ λέξει βαρβαρίζειν in Aristotle *SE* 165b20.

[26] See Geham 1914.37–40, 43–46; Rotolo 1972.403–404.

[27] Campos Daroca 1992.65–66.

[28] These include royal scribes or secretaries (*grammatistai*), especially the ones who read aloud the letters bearing the orders of the king at 3.128.5. Hollmann, who draws attention to this passage, observes that "just as *grammatistai* are machines converting signs from one medium to another, translators (ἑρμηνεῖς) in Herodotus transfer signs from one language to another" (the quotation is from Hollmann, forthcoming; but see also Hollmann 1998.207–209 and 223–224).

tate the work of Herodotus, so in the historical narrative they are a resource for royal inquiry.[29] As he prepares an expedition to conquer Ethiopia, Cambyses sends from Elephantine some Icthyophagi "who knew the Ethiopian language" to bring gifts to the Ethiopian king and investigate various matters, including the Table of the Sun (3.17, 18.1). These messengers answer the Ethiopian king's question about Persian culture, hear information about the Ethiopians, and inspect sites and burials. Their ethnic name "Fish-Eaters," which is the only thing we learn about them, positions them as intermediaries between the Persians and the other mainstream "bread-eating" societies on the one hand, and the meat-eating Ethiopians on the other.[30] Though they serve as instruments of Cambyses' aggressive designs, the innocent and respectful Icthyophagi are also, vis-à-vis the recipient of the *Histories*, surrogate-ethnographers for Herodotus himself.

The other linguistic interpreters in the *Histories*, called by their professional name, *hermēnees*, are colorless figures, but their rare appearances are signals that cultural issues are at stake. In one narrative the Samian Syloson once happened to make a gift to Darius of the bright red cloak he was wearing, which Darius had admired and asked to purchase. Somewhat unexpectedly, Darius rose to the throne and Syloson's trivial gesture turned out to have disproportionate consequences.[31] When the Samian presented himself to Darius and declared that he was the king's "benefactor" (*euergetēs*), his claim, translated into Persian, would have had greater import than the speaker perhaps intended or than the narrative conveys in Greek. The mention of interpreters (3.140.3) alludes to the official Persian title of *orosanga* of the king. In exchange for his early favor Syloson becomes tyrant of Samos, obtaining the same reward that in the next generation the Persian king will confer on another Samian, who fought with valor against the Greeks at Salamis.[32]

The last two sets of interpreters we must consider more deeply relate to the narrator's overall ideology in the sphere of language difference because they help to stage verbal exchanges where other discrepancies come into play that are more problematic than linguistic difference.[33] As the pyre is already

---

[29] See above, pp. 28–29.

[30] 3.20–25, esp. 22.4. Longo 1987.19–20. Fehling 1987.100. Rosellini and Saïd 1978.

[31] Van der Veen 1996.63, who also stresses the ambivalence of these consequences. Braund 1998.161–162.

[32] 8.85. See above, p. 57. For interpreters in this episode as evidence of the presence of Greeks at the Persian court, see Lewis 1985, esp. 105.

[33] Campos Daroca 1992.65.

blazing, Croesus remembers his past conversation with Solon and invokes Solon's name three times:

> Cyrus heard him and <u>bid the interpreters to ask Croesus</u> who was this man whose name he had called. They approached him and asked. Croesus was silent for a while, then, as he was being compelled, he answered, "One with whom I think it would be worth a lot of money for all tyrants to have a talk." Since what he said was unintelligible (ἄσημα) to them, they asked him again. At their insistence . . . Croesus explained how the Athenian Solon had come to him and, looking at his fortune, had made little of it. He repeated what Solon had told him and remarked how things had gone for him just as Solon had said at the time, speaking not so much for him (Croesus), but for the whole human race (ἐς ἅπαν τὸ ἀνθρώπινον), and especially for those who regard themselves fortunate... And Cyrus, <u>after hearing from the interpreters</u> what Croesus had said, changed his mind, reflecting that he himself was a human being (ἄνθρωπος) and was giving to the flames another human being (ἄλλον ἄνθρωπον); he therefore ordered that the pyre be extinguished as quickly as possible . . .
>
> 1.86.4–6

The reason why Croesus' words are unintelligible (*asēma*) to Cyrus at first is evidently not that they are spoken in Lydian. Interpreters are at hand, and that is all one needs for language.[34] The mention of interpreters at the beginning and at the end of this passage signals the overcoming of a more serious problem of communication between the two barbarian kings.[35] From a Greek viewpoint, Croesus is the philhellenic *barbaros* while Cyrus is the remote *barbaros*, who does not know Solon or anything else about Greece (see 1.153.1, cf. 5.73.2). Only after Croesus relates, and the interpreters translate, the whole story of Solon's visit to Croesus, Cyrus understands—as Croesus himself had not at the time—the "human" (*anthrōpinon*), that is to say, the cross-cultural, meaning of Solon's words. Solon is the real interpreter, who

---

[34] The scene between Cambyses and the defeated Psammenitus (3.14) is structurally analogous to this one but lacks the dimension of understanding or not understanding the hidden message of an utterance. Accordingly, no attention is drawn to language, and the role of intermediary, which in the scene with Croesus is fulfilled by interpreters, is assigned to an *angelos* ('messenger'), with no suggestion of linguistic translation (3.14.8).

[35] Hollmann 1998.221–222. Cf. also the Telmessians' interpretation of the snake-horse portent, that a host "of alien speech" (ἀλλόθροον) would come and overcome Croesus (1.78.3).

translates from the particular to the general, and his words are for the whole human race.[36]

The meaning of *anthrōpinos* as 'cross-cultural' in Herodotus is confirmed by the narrative of a verbal exchange inserted in the important series of generalizations at 3.38. This dialogue includes three sets of participants, each using three different types of cultural codes: a linguistic code, a code of communication (how things are said, including expressions and gestures), and a code of customs, the last representing the substance of the discourse. I quote the narrative partially in the context of the interpretive passage where it appears:[37]

> 1. If one should place all the *nomoi* in front of all men (πᾶσι ἀνθρώποισι) bidding them to choose the most beautiful, after examining them carefully each would choose his own. Indeed, all men (πάντες ἄνθρωποι) believe that their own *nomoi* are by far the best. . . . 2. That all men believe this one can see from many pieces of evidence (τεκμηρίοισι) among which the following: 3. Once during his reign Darius called some Greeks who were in the area and asked them how much money it would take for them to agree to eat their dead parents. The Greeks answered that they would not do that for anything. 4. Then Darius called some Callatian Indians, who are wont to eat their parents, and in the presence of the Greeks, <u>who understood through interpreters</u> what was being said, asked them how much money it would take for them to agree to burn their dead parents. They shouted out and bid him to refrain from blasphemy. Thus such things are set by custom νενόμισται and it seems to me that Pindar correctly said in poetry (ὀρθῶς . . . ποιῆσαι) that *Nomos* is king of all.

3.38.1–4

In this narrative, the cultural codes of communication stand out. The Persian Darius expresses himself in monetary terms, similar to those of his Lydian predecessor Croesus in the scene already considered ("for how much money"; cf. 1.86.4, "I think it would be worth a lot of money").[38] The Greeks respond, as we would say, in a "normal" way, and answer the question court-

---

[36] 1. 86.5, cf. 86.6. See Long 1987.111.

[37] For discussion of this chapter, see Gigante 1956.109–113; Humphreys 1987, Burkert 1988.21–22; Thomas 2000.125–127; Munson 1991.57–63 and 2001.168–172.

[38] The expressions in both cases reflect the quantitative mentality that Konstan 1987 describes as a characteristic of Persian kings.

room-style in the same terms in which it is asked. The Indians (and this is an orientalistic detail) display emotion. As for the code of customs, what the three parties are talking about is funeral rites, in which again each differs from the other two. Finally, the reference to interpreters draws attention to the languages—Persian, Greek and Callatian—specifying that the Greeks had the means to understand *these* codes, and that this item of difference is the least problematic of all.[39] At the level of the *nomoi*, sacred to the ones and repulsive to the others, the exchange reaches a dead end. *Cultural* "translation" is difficult when people find difference from themselves disturbing.

As Cyrus' understanding of Croesus can finally be achieved through one who speaks "for the whole human race," so here the understanding of the audience is made possible by the *histōr*. Darius' experiment with Greeks and Callatians provides the *tekmērion* (proof/sign) for the theoretical argument at 3.38.[40] Here Herodotus takes stock of his Greek contemporaries' belief that their own culture is superior and attributes a similar or even greater feeling to all other men (πάντες ἄνθρωποι). Cultural subjectivity is a sure thing, and it is both subjective and universal. As such, it indicates the objective validity and worth of all *nomoi*. Consequently, a higher principle of *Nomos* must exist from which these different but equally compelling *nomoi* all derive. And *Nomos*, unlike the different *nomoi*, unifies rather than separates men. Whether or not Herodotus is thinking in terms of the etymological correctness of names, he corroborates as *correct* (*orthōs*), the onomastic equivalence testified to by Pindar: "*Nomos* king of all."[41]

[39] Cf. Braund 1996.173. The fact that a Callatian Indian-to-Greek interpreter must have represented "surely a rare commodity" (Harrison 1998, ch. 2 "Herodotus' presentation of foreign languages") corroborates the argument that their presence is here symbolic.

[40] For the meaning of *tekmērion* in this and other Herodotean passages, see Hollmann 1998.4–6.

[41] Humphreys 1987.214. On onomastic correctness in Herodotus, see above, pp. 41–51. For a survey of the various meaning of *nomos* in different texts to the end of the fifth century, see Ostwald 1969.20–54. The distinction made here between *Nomos* and *nomoi* is that between men's universal (one would almost say "natural") impulse to regulate themselves in certain spheres of behavior (e.g. disposal of the dead) on the one hand and, on the other, the different forms of regulation (e.g. burial, cremation, etc.) that are produced by such an impulse in a given area of behavior in different societies. The gloss of corroboration of Pindar's phrase with gloss of opinion (ὀρθῶς μοι δοκέει) compensates for ποιῆσαι, a term for the fictions of poets which Herodotus tends to use critically. See Svenbro 1977.210. The interpretive resonance of the reference would be richer to us if we knew more about the meaning of the phrase in its original Pindaric context (fr. 169 SM); see Schroeder 1917, Stier 1928, Gigante 1956, Ostwald 1965, Humphreys 1987.

Language difference as paradigm

If the issue of language makes its fleeting appearance in the small narrative of Darius' inquiry only to advertise its own lack of importance, a certain correspondence is nevertheless established between the three types of codes simply because they are all culturally determined spheres of disagreement among the three speakers—different languages, different forms of expression, different customs. Language represents to Herodotus a particularly unproblematic area of difference; it therefore offers a paradigm of relativity to be extended as much as he possibly can to other spheres of culture in which difference is harder to accept as legitimate. The latter include, as here, funeral customs, but also diverging standards of justice and culture-specific knowledge about the gods. There even the narrator has to come to terms with his distaste for cannibalism, ritual prostitution, human sacrifice, and seemingly inadequate representations of the divine. I say "as much as he possibly can" because every observer is bound to be culturally subjective, as Herodotus himself theorizes (3.38.1), and several passages in the *Histories* show a not entirely resolved tension between relativism and evaluation. Herodotus is not, at any rate, the last ethnographer to be torn between the two.[42]

Herodotus' attempt, nevertheless, to extend the linguistic paradigm to a non-linguistic translation of culture is pervasive. It includes his application of the names of Greek gods to the gods of foreign peoples and his much discussed translations of the names of the gods, the latter combining in a special way linguistic and conceptual equivalence.[43] It particularly manifests itself at the formal level in certain glosses of ethnographic comparison which suggest an equivalence between an alien and a Greek practice, similar to the equivalences the narrator has no trouble in drawing between foreign and Greek words.[44] Through the narrative of Darius' experiment the translation of customs is made implicitly, between burning and eating the dead. Both linguistic and non-linguistic translations require considerable adjustment between discrepant phenomena: an Egyptian *baris* is a boat, but with special characteristics, just as the Callatian Indian version of what to the Greeks is a funeral. But the equivalence guarantees the intelligibility and legitimacy of the foreign phenomenon as another particular manifestation of *Nomos*, of which its Greek counterpart is also a manifestation.

---

[42] See e.g. 1.199, 2.64, 4.62, 4.93 for a discourse marked variously by the narrator's ambivalent reaction to cultural peculiarities in the areas we have mentioned.

[43] See above, pp. 11–12.

[44] E.g. 1.202.2 and 4.26.

Transcending culture

Nomos, in the Pindaric phrase as Herodotus uses it, transcends its individual embodiments—the *nomoi* of different peoples.[45] In a parallel way that almost suggests that the two concepts coincide, "the divine" manifests itself through the *theoi* worshipped by different peoples, but it transcends culture differentiation.[46] It is not surprising to find, therefore, that the divine also transcends the linguistic codes of the world, as those cases demonstrate in which oracles express themselves in different languages.

There are two cases of this phenomenon in the *Histories*, both accompanied by an extraordinary degree of metanarrative intervention.[47] The narrator advertises as something he regards a great wonder (θῶμά μοι μέγιστον) the experience of a certain Mys, a Carian who had been sent by Mardonius to consult various Greek oracles. When this Mys arrived at the sanctuary of Apollo Ptoos in Boeotia, the prophet (πρόμαντις) started to speak in a non-Greek language (βαρβάρῳ γλώσσῃ). Like the *histōr* who reports this story, so also the Thebans charged with writing down the response "were in wonder hearing a barbarian language instead of Greek." Mys snatched the tablet away from them and started making the transcription himself, saying that the oracle was speaking in Carian (8.135.1-3). The substance of the oracle is not given in this narrative, and the narrator says he has no knowledge of what precisely the consultation was about (8.133). What is important, and a wonder to him, is the demonstration of the cross-cultural value of divine utterances even when mediated by a cultural institution such as a sanctuary. *Barbarophōnoi*, in the words of oracles, are the Persian invaders of Greece (8.20.2; 9.43.3); but here their Carian envoy—himself one of the original *barbarophōnoi* of Homer—obtains direct access to the god.[48]

One episode in the *Histories* testifies to the internationalism of Delphic Apollo in the context of colonization, where the Greeks' unilateral ideology

[45] See above, p. 77 and note 41.

[46] On Herodotus' use of the words ὁ θεός and τὸ θεῖον, see Linforth 1928.

[47] For the oracles' linguistic mediation in connection with their international status, see Campos Daroca 1992.70–73, who also recalls the role of Dodona in the transmission of the names of the gods (2.52). See above p.13. But, aside from the two examples in Herodotus, we know of no other Greek oracle that expressed itself in a non-Greek language. See Parke and Wormell 1956; Fontenrose 1978.

[48] *Iliad* 2.867. See above, p. 2. There is no trace in Herodotus of Plutarch's interpretation of the prodigy as signifying that the oracle wished to communicate that the Greek language was not at the service of barbarians (*De defectu oraculorum* 412a; cf. *Aristides* 19). Lejeune 1940.48–57.

vis-à-vis native populations is well known.[49] In his account of the founding of Cyrene in Libya, the most linguistically foreign of lands,[50] Herodotus, like Pindar in his fourth Pythian ode, embraces the tradition that attributes to the *oikist* Battus the heroic disability of a weak or stuttering voice.[51] Again, like Pindar (*Pythian Odes* 4 and 5), Herodotus stresses the legitimacy of the position of Battus, whom Apollo's spontaneous oracle appointed as leader of the Theran expedition and king of the new foundation.[52] The two authors, however, operate in very different contexts. Pindar's praise of Battus is subordinated to the epinician glorification of his descendant Arcesilaus IV, the king of Cyrene in Pindar's own time.[53] By contrast, Herodotus recounts the foundation of Cyrene by Battus as a prelude to his history of that city's devolvement into discord and tyranny in the subsequent generations of Battiad rule.[54]

Other discrepancies between our two earliest sources on Battus are more important for their respective views on Greek and foreign speech. In Pindar, the founder of Cyrene is the civilizer of a barbarian land, who scares off the deep-roaring (βαρυκόμποι) Libyan lions with his "overseas language" (γλῶσσαν … ὑπερποντίαν). Battus' stuttering speech, in other words, becomes effective in the new setting on account of the divine voice of Delphi, which prescribed the settlement, and thanks to the superior political power of the Greek language in relation to the animal voice of the natives.[55] A version of Apollo's oracle to Battus that appears in Diodorus translates Pindar's metaphor into literal terms:

---

[49] See Moggi 1991.35, 40n29, where the examples of exceptional recognition of the role of foreign populations are all from Herodotus.

[50] Libya is the land of the Atarantes, who have no personal names 4.184.2–3; of the troglodytes who speak like bats (4.183.4); of the encounter between Nasamones and pygmies (2.32.6); and of the silent transactions between Carthaginians and Libyans. Campos Daroca 1992.74, 128.

[51] Pindar *Pythian Odes* 4.62: δυσθρόου φωνᾶς. Herodotus 4.155.1: ἰσχνόφωνος καὶ τραυλός. For Battus' disability in the context of the morphological category of the hero, see Giangiulio 1981; Cosi 1987; Calame 1993.143–144. For a survey of the traditions about Cyrene, see Gentili 1990; Calame 1996.

[52] *Pythian Odes* 4.61–62: αὐτομάτῳ κελάδῳ; cf. *Pythian Odes* 4.5–6. Herodotus 4.155.

[53] Dougherty 1993.107–117; Calame 1996.116–128. *Pythian Odes* 5 and 4 both celebrate the victory of Arcesilaus' brother in law in 462. The colonization themes in these odes refer back to Pindar's earlier Cyrenaic ode, *Pythian Odes* 9 (474 BC), especially the section on the marriage of Apollo with the nymph Cyrene (5–69). Dougherty 1993.147.

[54] For the anti-Battiad thrust of Herodotus' narrative, see Chamoux 1953.207; Laronde 1990.35–37.

[55] *Pythian Odes* 5.55–59; cf. the rationalized version of Paus. 10.5.7. Dougherty 1993.107. Pindar's episode about Battus overcoming the lions with his voice recontextualizes the mythical tradition of the nymph Cyrene wrestling a lion barehanded (*Pythian Odes* 9.26–28). Cosi 1987.132–133; Dougherty 1992.147.

O Battus, you came for your voice, but Phoebus Apollo the Lord
Sends you to lovely-crowned Libya,
To rule over broad Cyrene and enjoy royal privilege.
There, when you set foot in Libya, <u>skin-clad barbarian men</u>
<u>Will come against you</u>; but you pray to the son of Cronus
And gray-eyed Pallas who rouses the battle and the son of Zeus,
The unshorn Phoebus, and you will hold victory in your hand.
And blessed over lovely-crowned Libya you shall rule,
Both you and your dynasty. Your guide is Phoebus Apollo.

Diodorus 8.29[56]

Herodotus gives his colonization narrative a different emphasis. Neither he nor the oracles he reports mention confrontations of the Greek colonists with lions or native peoples. His Battus is a reluctant leader—not a bad thing in Herodotus—whose hesitancy is perhaps symbolized by his stutter.[57] Battus, who doubts his power and strength, finally goes overseas in obedience to the oracle and founds the city in Libya after two false starts and a great deal of trouble (4.155.4; 156–157). He moves his settlement once within Libya, under the sponsorship (and control) of the local Libyans. He reigns for forty years apparently without waging any wars or conquering anyone.[58] In Herodotus' narrative, trouble with the local Libyans only begins under Battus II (4.159) and intensifies with Arcesilaus II. The analogue of Battus the stutterer is his fourth successor, Battus III the Lame, who is also apparently reluctant to rule: in some sense he re-founds the city by promoting, according to a Delphic prescription, a quasi-democratic form of government in Cyrene. But the next king, the third Arcesilaus, undoes the reform, and the dynasty marches on to its final ruin.

In relation to Pindar and other sources on the colonization of Cyrene—as well as, we might add, Greek colonization in general—Herodotus' narrative presents a striking peculiarity. On the one hand, it reports no fewer than four Delphic oracles that order the Greeks to colonize Libya. On the other hand it also strives to legitimize the foundation not only from a Greek but also from

---

[56] At 8.30 a Delphic oracle to Arcesilaus reproaches the kings of Cyrene for causing the anger of the gods because they did not rule in the manner of Battus.

[57] The model of the unambitious leader is Leonidas, who did not expect to become king (7.205.1). For the deformity of Battus in the context of traditional stories of colonization, see Giangiulio 1981; Vernant 1981; Cosi 1987.

[58] 4.159.1. For evidence, outside of Herodotus, of Battus' wars with the natives and buildings of other settlements, see Malkin 1994.174 and note 13.

a barbarian viewpoint.[59] It does so, moreover, in a context that exploits the Pindaric themes of Battus' disability, the voice of the oracle, and the issue of Greek versus native speech. In Herodotus' scene of Battus' consultation of the oracle, Apollo, Battus, and Herodotus' Greek sources engage in a complicated dialogue that is, at one level, about language. Louder than everyone else's is the voice of the narrator himself, who interferes at every sentence as the interpreter of the Delphic god:

> After some time a child was born whose speech was defective and halting, to whom they gave the name Battus ['Stammerer'], as the Thereans and the Cyreneans say, but in my opinion some other name: he changed his name to Battus after he came to Libya, taking this name as a result of the oracle he received at Delphi and of the honor he was granted there. For *battos* in Libyan means 'king' (*basileus*), and for this reason I think the Pythia addressed to him in the Libyan tongue, knowing that he would be king in Libya. For when he became a man, he went to Delphi about his voice, and the Pythia prophesied to him as follows:
>
> "O Battus, you came for your voice (*phōnē*), but Phoebus Apollo the Lord sends you as *oikist* in sheep-nurturing Libya," just as she would have said in Greek "O king, you came about your voice."

4.155.1–3

Herodotus' translation from the Libyan refashions the Therean and Cyrenaic tradition he himself reports.[60] It also reverses the pattern, testified in other sources, of "bilingual" oracles appropriating foreign phenomena to the Greek language. In one of the foundation stories, for example, Delphi prescribes that the Sicilian city be named "Gela" (a local name) after the "laughter" (*gelas*) of

---

[59] Calame 1993.141. Scholars currently tend to think that the native populations played a more important role in Cyrenaica than in other areas colonized by the Greeks. Laronde 1990.48. Giannini 1990.70–71.

[60] Dougherty 1993 sees an allusion to the Libyan meaning in Pindar's "automatic" oracle, which is similar to the oracle reported by Herodotus (*Pythian Odes* 4.59–63). However, Herodotus' explicit translation is unique in early sources (it occurs later in a scholium on Pindar, Drachmann 1984.2:93, and Hesychius s.v. Βάττος), and he presents it as not generally known.

the future *oikist*.[61] With "Battus," on the contrary, the *histōr* insists in his own voice that the name by which the Greek founder of Cyrene is most commonly known is a Libyan word because the god who elected him king in Libya "named" him "King" in the local tongue.[62]

Unlike Herodotus, the Therean and Cyrenaeans who preserve the foundation story derive the name Battus from the Greek word *battarizō* (βατταρίζω 'stutter'). They identify the *oikist* with a linguistic handicap that corresponds to his social and political marginality in a Greek context:[63] he is the natural son of a Theran citizen and his Cretan concubine, and therefore not fully an insider, not endowed with a strong "voice" in the *polis* and, one can almost say, not fully Greek. To this interpretation, which makes *Battos* (Battus) onomatopoeically and semantically analogous to *barbaros*,[64] Herodotus' Apollo responds with the equivalence of *Battos* and *basileus*. The issue of Battus' voice (*phōnē*) is really one of language.

The Thereans and Cyrenaeans, who fail to learn from the oracle the real significance of Battus' ominous name—and perhaps, therefore, misunderstand the task of colonization—resemble the Perinthians, who sing the *paion* oblivious to the language of the Paeonians. They only hear pure Greek as conveying meaning.[65] They are to this day as presumptuously ignorant of foreign realities as were the Theran colonists, who first settled in the wrong place. When they consulted Delphi again, complaining that they had colonized Libya and were not better off, the oracle chided with Dorian-colored and punning speech: "If you know, not having been there Libya nurturer of flocks better than I who have been there, I indeed admire your wisdom" (4.159.3). The *histōr* of the *Histories* has also been there. Because he moves across languages, he is also uniquely qualified to understand the utterances of the divine. His message is about different cultures and concerns "all men."

---

[61] Stephanus of Byzantium s.v. Γέλα; *Etymologicum Magnum* 225. Parke and Wormell 1956.2.166. On bilingual oracles, see Dougherty 1992.45–48, with this and other examples.

[62] Herodotus does not mention Battus' alternative name, Aristoteles, known from Pindar (*Pythian Odes* 5.87) and other sources.

[63] Campos Daroca 1992.128. Calame 1996.136.

[64] Cosi 1987.121,130.

[65] In this case, from our point of view, they were apparently right: see Masson 1976, who argues that the name Battus appears in different parts of Greece, is really Greek and derives from βατταρίζω.

BIBLIOGRAPHY

Alty, J. 1982. "Dorians and Ionians." *JHS* 102:1–14.

Armayor, O. K. 1987. "Hecataeus' Humor and Irony in Herodotus' Narrative of Egypt." *AW* 16:11–18.

———. 1978. "Herodotus' Persian Vocabulary." *AW* 1:4.

Asad, T. 1986. "The Concept of Cultural Translation in British Social Anthropology." In Clifford and Marcus 1986:141–164.

Asheri, D. 1988a. *Erodoto: la Lidia e la Persia. Libro I delle Storie.* Milan.

———. 1988b. "Herodotus on Thracian Society and History." In *Hérodote et les peuples non grecs.* Entretiens XXXV. Fondation Hardt (ed. G. Nenci) 131–163. Geneva.

———. 1990. *Erodoto: la Persia. Libro III delle Storie.* Milan.

Asheri, D., and A. Corcella, eds. 2003. *Erodoto, Le storie. Libro VIII.* With commentary adjourned by P. Vannicelli and translation by A. Fraschetti. Milan.

Bacon, H. 1961. *Barbarians in Greek Tragedy.* New Haven.

Badian, E. 1994. "Herodotus on Alexander I of Macedon." In Hornblower 1994:107–127.

Baldry, H. C. 1965. *The Unity of Mankind in Greek Thought.* Cambridge.

Bailey, N. 1983. *The Innocent Anthropologist.* London.

Bal, M. 1985. *Narratology: Introduction to the Theory of Narrative.* Toronto, Buffalo, and London.

Bakhtin, M. M. 1981. *The Dialogic Imagination.* Ed. M. Holoquist. Trans. C. Emerson and M. Holoquist. Austin, TX.

Barney, R. *Names and Nature in Plato's Cratylus.* New York and London.

Baxter, T. M. S. 1992. *The Cratylus: Plato's Critique of Naming.* Philosophia antiqua 58. Leiden and New York.

Benardete, S. 1969. *Herodotean Inquiries.* The Hague.

Benveniste, E. 1966. "Rélations léxicales entre la Perse et la Grèce ancienne." Atti del convegno sul tema: la Persia e il mondo greco-romano. *Problemi Attuali di Scienza e di Cultura* 76:479–485. Rome.

Bernabò, L. 1977. "Oracoli come messaggio: Erodoto testimone di una dimensione orale dei responsi oracolari?" *BIFG* 4:157–174.

Bertelli, L. 2001. "Hecataeus: From Genealogy to Historiography." In Luraghi 2001:67–94.

Boedeker, D., ed. 1987. *Herodotus and the Invention of History. Arethusa* 20.1/2.

Booth, W. C. 1983. *The Rhetoric of Fiction.* 2nd edition. Chicago.

Bracht Branham, R. 2002. *Bakhtin and the Classics.* Evanston.

Braund, D. 1998. "Herodotus and the Problematics of Reciprocity." In *Reciprocity in Ancient Greece* (eds. C. Gill, N. Postlethwaite, and R. Seaford) 159–180. Oxford.

Briant, P. 1988. "Hérodote et la société perse." In *Hérodote et les peuples non grecs.* Entretiens XXXV. Fondation Hardt (ed. G. Nenci) 69–104. Geneva.

Broadhead, H. D., ed. 1960. *The Persae of Aeschylus.* Cambridge.

Brown, F. S., and W. B. Tyrell. 1985. "ἐκτιλώσαντο: A Reading of Herodotus' Amazons." *CJ* 80:297–302.

Burkert, W. 1970. "La genèse des choses et des mots: le Papyrus Derveni entre Anaxagore et Cratyle." *Les Études philosophiques* 25:443–453.

———. 1985. "Herodot über die Namen der Götter. Polytheismus als historisches Problem." *MH* 43:121–132.

———. 1988. "Herodot als Historiker fremden Religionen." In *Hérodote et les peuples non grecs.* Entretiens XXXV. Fondation Hardt (ed. G. Nenci) 69–104. Geneva.

Calame, C. 1996. *Mythe et histoire dans l'antiquité grecque: la création symbolique d'une colonie.* Lausanne.

Campos Daroca, J. 1992. *Experiencias del Lenguaje en las Historias de Hérodoto.* Almeria.

Cardona, G. R. 1976. *Introduzione all'etnolinguistica.* Bologna.

Cartledge, P. 1993. *The Greeks: A Portrait of Self and Others.* Oxford.

Castriota, D. 2000. "Justice, Kingship, and Imperialism: Rhetoric and Reality in Fifth-Century B. C. Representations Following the Persian Wars." In Cohen 2000:443–479.

Chamberlain, D. 1999. "On Atomics Onomastic and Metarhythmic Translations in Herodotus." *Arethusa* 32.3:263–312.

Chamoux, F. 1953. *Cyrène sous la monarchie des battiades.* Paris.

Chantraine, P. 1968–1980. *Dictionnaire étymologique de la langue grecque.* Paris.

Chatman, S. 1978. *Story and Discourse: Narrative Structure in Fiction and Film.* Ithaca, NY.

Christ, M. R. 1994. "Herodotean Kings and Historical Inquiry." *CA* 13/2:167–202.

Classen, C. J. 1976. "The Study of Language amongst Socrates' Contemporaries." In *Sophistik* (ed. C. J. Classen) 215–247. Darmstadt.

Clifford, J., and G. E. Marcus. 1986. *Writing Culture: The Poetics and Politics of Ethnography.* Berkeley, Los Angeles, and London.

Cobet, J. 1971. *Herodots Exkurse und die Frage der Einheit seines Werke.* Historia Einzelschriften 17. Wiesbaden.

Cohen, B., ed. 2000. *Not the Classical Ideal: Athens and the Construction of the Other in Greek Art.* Leiden.

Cole, T. 1990. *Democritus and the Sources of Greek Anthropology.* American Philological Association Monograph Series 25. Atlanta.

Coleman, J. E. 1997. "Ancient Greek Ethnocentrism." In Coleman and Waltz 1997:175–220.

Coleman, J. E., and C. A. Waltz, eds. 1997. *Greeks and Barbarians: Essays on the Interaction between Greeks and non-Greeks in Antiquity and the Consequences for Eurocentrism.* Bethesda, MD.

Colvin, S. 1999. *Dialect in Aristophanes.* Oxford.

Connor, W. R. 1993a. "The Ionian Era of Athenian Civic Identity." *Am. Philos. Soc.* 137:194–206.

———. 1993b. "The *Histōr* in History." In Rosen and Farrell 1993:127–140.

Cook, A. B. 1907. "Nomen Omen." *CR* 21:169.

Cosi, D. M. 1987. "Jammed Communication: Battos, the Founder of Cyrene, Stammering and Castrated." In *The Regions of Silence: Studies on the Difficulty of Communicating* (ed. M. G. Ciani). Amsterdam.

Corcella, A. 1984. *Erodoto e l'analogia.* Palermo.

———. 1993. *Erodoto: La Scizia e la Libia. Libro IV delle Storie.* Milan.

Darbo-Peschanski, C. 1987. *Le discours du particulier. Essai sur l'enquête Hérodotéenne.* Paris.

Derow, P., and R. Parker. 2003. *Herodotus and His World. Essays from a Conference in Memory of George Forrest.* Oxford.

David, E. 1999. "Sparta's Kosmos of Silence." In *Sparta: New Perspectives* (eds. A. Hodkinson and A. Powell) 117–146. London.

De Jong, I. J. F. 1987. *Narrators and Focalizers: The Presentation of the Story in the Iliad.* Amsterdam.

———. 1998. "Aspects Narratologiques des Histoires d'Hérodote." *Lalies. Actes des sessions de linguistique et de littérature* 19.

Detienne, M. 1973. *Les maîtres de la verité dans la Grèce archaïque.* Paris.

———. 1977. *The Gardens of Adonis: Spices in Greek Mythology.* Trans. Janet Lloyd. New York, repr. Princeton 1994. [Paris 1972].

Detienne, M., and J. P. Vernant. 1989. *The Cuisine of Sacrifice among the Greeks.* Trans. P. Wissung. Chicago. [Paris 1979].

Dewald, C. 1981. "Women and Culture in Herodotus' Histories." *Women's Studies* 8.1/2:93–126.

———. 1987. "Narrative Surface and Authorial Voice in Herodotus' *Histories.*" In Boedeker 1987:147–170.

———. 1993. "Reading the World: The Interpretation of Objects in Herodotus' *Histories.*" In Rosen and Farrell 1993:55–70.

———. 1998. *Herodotus. The Histories.* Trans. Robin Waterfield, with an Introduction and notes by Carolyn Dewald. Oxford.

Diels, H. 1910. "Die Anfänge der Philologie bei den Griechen." In *Neue Jahrbücher für das klassische Altertum, Geschichte und deutsche Literatur* 25.13:1–25. [Repr. in H. Diels, *Kleine Schriften zur Geschiche der antiken Philosophie.* Hildesheim 1969:68–92].

Diller, H. 1961. "Die Hellenen-Barbaren-Antithese im Zeitalter der Persekriege." In *Grecs et Barbares.* Entretiens VIII. Fondation Hardt. Geneva. 39–68.

Donadoni, S. 1947. "Erodoto, Plutarco e l'Egitto." *Belfagor* 2:203–208.

———. 1986. *Cultura dell'Antico Egitto.* Rome.

Dougherty, C. 1993. *The Poetics of Colonization: From City to Text in Archaic Greece.* Oxford.

———. 1996. "Democratic Contradictions and the Synoptic Illusion of Euripides' Ion." In Ober and Hedrick 1996:249–270.

Dover, K., ed. 1993. *Aristophanes: Frogs.* Oxford.

Dubois, P. 1982. *Centaurs and Amazons: Women and the Pre-History of the Great Chain of Being.* Ann Arbor.

Dué, C. 2005. *The Captive Woman's Lament in Greek Tragedy.* Austin, TX.

Evans, J. A. S. 1985. "Caudaules Whom the Greeks Name Myrsilos." *GRBS* 26:229–233.

———. 1991. *Herodotus Explorer of the Past.* Princeton.

Farina, A., ed. 1963. *Ipponatte. Introduzione, testo critico, testimonianze, traduzione.* Naples.

Fehling, D. 1989. *Herodotus and his 'Sources': Citation, Invention and Narrative Art.* Trans. J. G. Howie. Leeds. [Berlin and New York 1971].

Fetterman, D. M. 1989. *Ethnography Step by Step.* Newbury Park, CA.

Finley, M. I. 1975. *The Use and Abuse of History.* New York.

Flory, S. 1987. *The Archaic Smile of Herodotus.* Detroit.

Flower, M. A., and J. Marincola, eds. 2002. *Herodotus Histories: Book IX.* Cambridge.

Fontenrose, J. 1978. *The Delphic Oracle: Its Responses and Operations with a Catalogue of Responses.* Berkeley, Los Angeles, and London.

Forbes, P. B. R. 1933. "Greek Pioneers in Philology and Grammar." *CR* 47:105–112.

Fornara, C. W. 1971. *Herodotus. An Interpretive Essay.* Oxford.

———. 1983. *The Nature of History in Ancient Greece and Rome.* Berkeley, Los Angeles, and London.

Fowler, R. L. 1996. "Herodotos and his Contemporaries." *JHS* 116:62–87.

Friis Johansen, H., and E. W. Whittle, eds. 1980. *Aeschylus. The Suppliants.* 3 vols. Copenhagen.

Froidefond, C. 1971. *Le mirage égyptien dans la littérature grecque d'Homère à Aristote.* Paris.

Geertz, C. 1973. *The Interpretation of Cultures.* New York.

Gehman, H. S. 1914. *The Interpreters of Foreign Languages Among the Ancients.* Diss. Lancaster, PA.

Genette, G. 1980. *Narrative Discourse: An Essay in Method.* Foreword by J. Culler. [Paris 1972].

Gentili, B., ed. 1990. *Cirene: storia, mito e letteratura.* Urbino.

Georges, P. 1994. *Barbarian Asia and the Greek Experience*. Baltimore and London.

Giannini, P. 1990. "Cirene nella poesia greca: tra mito e storia." In Gentili 1990:51–95.

Gigante, M. 1956. *Nomos Basileus*. Naples.

Goldhill, S. 1990. "The Great Dionysia and Civic Ideology." In *Nothing to do with Dionysos?* (eds. J. Winkler and F. Zeitlin) 1990:97–129. Princeton.

Gould, J. 1989. *Herodotus*. London.

———. 1991. "Give and Take in Herodotus." *The Fifteenth J. L. Meyers Memorial Lecture*. Oxford.

Grene, D., trans. 1987. *Herodotus, the History*. Chicago and London.

Griffiths, A. "Kissing Cousins: Some Curious Cases of Adjacent Material in Herodotus." In Luraghi 2001:161–178.

Güntert, H. 1921. *Von der Sprache der Götter und Geister*. Halle.

Guthrie, W. H. C. 1965. *A History of Greek Philosophy II*. Cambridge.

———. 1969. *A History of Greek Philosophy III*. Cambridge.

———. 1971. *The Sophists*. Cambridge.

Hainsworth, J. B. 1967. "Greek Views of Greek Dialectology." *Transactions of the Philological Society, Oxford*. 62–76.

Hall, E. 1989. *Inventing the Barbarian: Greek Self-Definition Through Tragedy*. Oxford.

———, ed. 1996. *Aeschylus. Persians*. Warminster.

———. 2002. "When is a Myth not a Myth?" In Harrison 2002:133–152. [Reprinted from *Arethusa* 25.1992:181–201; also in Lefkowitz and Rogers 1996:333–348].

Hall, J. M. 1995. "The Role of Language in Greek Ethnicities." *PCPS* 41:83–100.

———. 1997. *Ethnic Identity in Greek Antiquity*. Cambridge.

———. 2002. *Hellenicity: Between Ethnicity and Culture*. Chicago.

Hansen, M. H.1996. "The Ancient Athenian and the Modern Liberal View of Liberty as a Democratic Ideal." In Ober and Hedrick 1996:91–104.

Harrison, T. 1998. "Herodotus' Conception of Foreign Languages." *Histos* 2. http://www.dur.ac.uk/Classics/histos/1998/harrison.html.

———. 2000. *Divinity and History: The Religion of Herodotus*. Oxford.

———, ed. 2002. *Greeks and Barbarians*. New York.

Hartog, F. 1988. *The Mirror of Herodotus: The Representation of the Other in the Writing of History*. Trans. J. Lloyd. Berkeley, Los Angeles, and London. [Paris 1980].

Harmatta, J. 1990. "Herodotus, Historian of the Cimmerians and the Scythians." *Hérodote et les peuples non-grecs*. Entretiens XXXV. Fondation Hardt (ed. G. Nenci) 115–130. Geneva.

Heidel, W. A. 1935. "Hecataeus and the Egyptian Priests in Herodotus, Book II." *American Academy of Arts and Sciences*. 18.2:59, 63.

Heinimann, F. 1945/1965. *Nomos und Physis*. Basel.

Hollmann, A. 1998. *The Master of Signs: Signs and Signification in the Histories of Herodotos*. Diss. Harvard University.

———. 2000. "*Epos* as Authoritative Speech in Herodotos' *Histories*." *HSCP* 2000:207–225.

———. Forthcoming. "The Manipulation of Signs in Herodotus' *Histories*."

Hornblower, S., ed. 1994. *Greek Historiography*. Oxford.

———. 2000. "Personal Names and the Study of the Ancient Greek Historians." In Hornblower and Matthews 2000:129–143.

———. 2003. "Panionios of Chios and Hermotimos of Pedasa (Hdt. 8.104–6)." In Derow and Parker 2003:37–57.

Hornblower, S., and E. Matthews, eds. 2000. *Greek Personal Names: Their Value as Evidence*. Oxford.

How, W. W., and J. Wells. 1928. *A Commentary on Herodotus*. 2 vols. Oxford (repr. 1964).

Hude, C., ed. 1927. *Herodoti Historiae*. Oxford.

Humphreys, S. 1987. "Law, Custom and Culture in Herodotus." In Boedeker 1987:211–220.

Hunter, V. 1982. *Past and Process in Herodotus and Thucydides*. Princeton.

Immerwahr, H. R. 1966. *Form and Thought in Herodotus*. Cleveland.

Isaac, B. *The Invention of Racism in Classical Antiquity*. Princeton.

Jacoby, F. 1913. "Herodotus." In *Realencyclopadie der classischen Altertumswissenschaft* (eds. Pauly-Wissowa-Kroll) Supplement 2:250–520.

———. 1955. *Die Fragmente der griechischen Historiker. III Geschichte von Städten und Völkern (Horographie und Ethnographie), b Kommentar zur Nr. 297–607*, 2 vols. Leiden.

Janssen, T. H. 1984. *Timotheus, Persae: A Commentary*. Amsterdam.

Jones, C. P. 1996. "ἔθνος and γένος in Herodotus." *CQ* 46:315–320.

Kahn, C. H. 1979. *The Art and Thought of Heraclitus: An Edition of the Fragments with Translation and Commentary*. Cambridge.

———. 1997. "Was Euthyphro the Author of the Derveni Papyrus?" In Laks and Most 1997:55–63.

Kerferd, G. B. 1981. *The Sophistic Movement*. Cambridge.

Kirchberg, L. 1965. *Die Funtion der Orakel im Werke Herodots*. Göttigen.

Klees, H. 1964. *Die Eigenart des griechischen Glaubens an Oraekel und Seher*. Stuttgart.

Konstan, D. 1987. "Persians, Greeks, and Empire." In Boedeker 1987:59–70.

Kothe, H. 1969. "Der Skythenbegriff bei Herodot." *Klio* 51:15–88.

Kraus, M. 1987. *Name und Sache: Ein Problem in frühgriechischen Denken*. Amsterdam.

Kretzmann, N. 1971. "Plato on the Correctness of Names." *American Philosophical Quarterly* 8/2:126–138.

Laks, A., and G. W. Most. 1997. *Studies in the Derveni Papyrus*. Oxford.

Lanza, D. 1979. *Lingua e discorso nell'Atene delle professioni*. Naples.

Laronde, A. 1990. "Cyrène sous les derniers Battiades." In Gentili 1990:35–50.

Lateiner, D. 1987. "Nonverbal Communication in the Histories of Herodotus." In Boedeker 1987.

———. 1989. *The Historical Method of Herodotus*. Toronto, Buffalo, and London.

Lattimore, R. 1939. "Herodotus and the Names of the Egyptian Gods." *CP* 34:357–365.

Laurot, B. 1981. "Idéaux Grecs et barbarie chez Hérodote." *Ktema* 6:39–48.

Lazzeroni, R. 1957. "Lingua degli dei e lingua degli uomini." *ASNP* 2/26:2–25.

Lefkowitz, M., and G. M. Rogers, eds. 1996. *Black Athena Revisited*. Chapel Hill.

Legrand, E. 1932. *Hérodote: Introduction*. Paris.

———, ed. 1946–1948. *Hérodote*. vols. 2–11. Paris.

Lejeune, M. 1940–1948. "La curiosité linguistique dans l'antiquité classique." *Conférences de l'Institut de Linguistique de l'Université de Paris* 8:45–61.

Levin, S. B. 1995. "What's in a Name: A Reconsideration of the *Cratylus'* Historical Sources and Topics." *Ancient Philosophy* 15:91–115.

———. 1997. "Greek Conception of Naming: Three Forms of Appropriateness in Plato and the Literary Tradition." *CP* 92:46–57.

Levy, E. 1984. "Naissance du concept de barbare." *Ktema* 9:5–14.

———. 1991. "Hérodote philobarbaros ou la vision du barbare chez Hérodote." In *L'étranger dans le monde grec II. Actes du Deuxième Colloque sur l'Étranger* (ed. R. Lonis) 193–244. Nancy.

Lewis, D. H. 1985. "Persians in Herodotus." In *The Greek Historians: Literature and History. Papers presented to A. E. Raubitschek* (ed. A. E. Raubitschek) 101–117. Saratoga, California.

Linforth, I. M. 1926. "Greek Gods and Foreign Gods in Herodotus." *UCPCPh* 9:1–25. [Repr. in Linforth 1987:47–71].

———. 1928. "Named and Unnamed Gods in Herodotus." *UCPCPh* 9:201–243. [Repr. in Linforth 1987:77–93].

———. 1940. "Greek and Egyptian Gods (Herodotus II.50 and 52)." *CP* 35:300–301. [Repr. in Linforth 1987:72–73].

———. 1987. *Studies in Herodotus and Plato.* Edited with an introduction by L. Tarán. London.

Lloyd, A. B. 1975. *Herodotus Book II Introduction.* Leiden.

———. 1976. *Herodotus Book II. Commentary 1–98.* Leiden.

———. 1988. *Herodotus Book II. Commentary 99–182.* Leiden.

———. 1988a. "Herodotus on Egyptians and Libyans." *Hérodote et les Peuples non Grecs.* Entretiens XXXV. Fondation Hardt (ed. G. Nenci) 215–244. Geneva.

Lloyd, G. E. R. 1966. *Polarity and Analogy: Two Types of Argumentation in Early Greek Thought.* Cambridge.

Long. T. 1984. *Babarians in Greek Comedy.* Carbondale and Edwardsville, IL.

Longo, O. 1987. "I mangiatori di pesce: regime alimentare e quadro culturale." *Materiali e discussioni per l'analisi dei testi classici* 18:9–55.

Loraux, N. 1986. *The Invention of Athens: The Funeral Oration in the Classical City.* Trans. A. Sheridan. Cambridge, MA. [Paris 1981].

———. 1993. *The Children of Athena: Athenian Ideas about Citizenship and the Division between the Sexes.* Trans. C. Levine. Princeton. [Paris 1984].

———. 2002. *The Mourning Voice: An Essay on Greek Tragedy.* Trans. E. Trapnell Rawlings; foreword by P. Pucci. Ithaca, NY.

Luraghi, N., ed. 2001. *The Historian's Craft in the Age of Herodotus.* Oxford.

Macan, R. W. 1895. *Herodotus: the Fourth, Fifth and Sixth Books*. 2 vols. London. [Repr. New York 1973].

——. 1908. *Herodotus. The Seventh, Eighth and Ninth Books*. 2 vols. London.

Malkin, I. 1987. *Religion and Colonization in Ancient Greece*. Leiden.

——. 1994. *Myth and Territory in the Spartan Mediterranean*. Cambridge.

——, ed. 2001. *Ethnic Perceptions of Greek Ethnicity*. Cambridge, MA and London.

——. Forthcoming. "Postcolonial Concepts and Ancient Greek Colonization." *Modern Language Quarterly*.

Mandell, S. 1990. "The Language, Eastern Sources, and Literary Posture of Herodotus." *AW* 21:103–108.

Marincola, J. 1987. "Herodotean Narrative and the Narrator's Presence." In Boedeker 1987:121–138.

Masaracchia, A. 1978. *Erodoto: la Sconfitta dei Persiani. Libro IX delle Storie*. Milan.

Masson, O. 1976. "Le nom de Battos, fondateur de Cyrène, et un group de mots grecs apparentés." *Glotta* 54:84–98.

McGready, A. G. 1968. "Egyptian Words in Greek Vocabulary." *Glotta* 46:247–254.

McNeal, R. A. 1985. "How did the Pelasgians Become Hellenes? Herodotus 1.56–58." *ICS* X.1:11–21.

Merkelbach, R. 1982. "Der Orfische Papyrus von Derveni." *ZPE* 1:1–12.

Meyer, E. 1862. *Forschungen zur alten Geschichte* I. Halle. [Repr. Hildesheim 1966].

Mikalson, J. 2003. *Herodotus and Religion in the Persian Wars*. Ann Arbor.

Miller, M. C. 1997. *Athens and Persia: A Study in Cultural Receptivity*. Cambridge.

Mitchell, L. G. 1997. *Greeks Bearing Gifts: The Public Use of Private Relationships*. Cambridge.

Moggi, M. 1991. "Greci e barbari: Uomini e no." In *Civiltà classica e mondo dei barbari* (ed. L. de Finis) 31–46. Trent.

Momigliano, A. D. 1975. *Alien Wisdom: The Limits of Hellenization*. Cambridge.

——. 1975a. "The Fault of the Greeks." *Daedalus* 104/2:1–15.

Mora, F. 1985. *Religione e Religioni nelle Storie di Erodoto*. Milan.

Morpurgo Davies, A. 2000. "Greek Personal Names and Linguistic Continuity." In Hornblower and Matthews 2000:15–39.

———. 2002. "The Greek Notion of Dialect." In Harrison 2002:153–171. [Reprinted from *Verbum* 10:7–27 (1987)].

Morris, I. 1996. "The Strong Principle of Equality and the Archaic Origins of Greek Democracy." In Ober and Hedrick 1996:19–48.

Mosley, D. J. 1971. "Greeks, Barbarians, Language and Contact." *AS* 2:1–6.

Müller, K. E. 1972. *Geschichte der antiken Ethographie und ethnologischen Theoriebildung I.* Wiesbaden.

Müller, R. 1980. "Hellene und 'Barbaren' in der griechischen Philosophie." *Menschenbild und Humanismus der Antike. Studien zur Geschichte Literatur und Philosphie.* Leipzig.

Munson, R. V. 1991. "The Madness of Cambyses (Herodotus 3.16–38)." *Arethusa* 24:43–65.

———. 1993. "Three Aspects of Spartan Kingship in Herodotus." In Rosen and Farrell 1993:39–54.

———. 2001. *Telling Wonders: Ethnographic and Political Discourse in the Work of Herodotus.* Ann Arbor.

Murray, G., ed. 1955. *Aeschyli Tragoediae.* Oxford.

Myres, J. L. 1907. "A History of the Pelasgian Theory." *JHS* 27:170–225.

Nagy, G. 1976. "The Name of Achilles: Etymology and Epic." In *Studies in Greek Italic and Indo-European Linguistics: Offered to Leonard R. Palmer* (ed. A. Davies and W. Meid) 209–237. Innsbruck.

———. 1988. "Herodotus the *Logios*." In Boedeker 1988:175–84.

———. 1990. *Pindar's Homer: The Lyric Possession of an Epic Past.* Baltimore and London.

Nesselrath, H.-G. 1999. "Dodona, Siwa und Herodot." *MH* 56/1:1–14

Nenci, G. 1994. *Erodoto: la rivolta della Ionia. V Libro delle Storie.* Milan.

Nippel, W. 2002. "The Construction of the 'Other'." Trans. A. Nevill. In Harrison 2002:278–310. [Originally published in S. Settis, ed., *I Greci*, vol. 1, *Noi e i Greci.* Turin 1996:165–196].

Ober, J., and C. Hedrick, eds. 1996. *Demokratia: A Conversation on Democracies Ancient and Modern.* Princeton.

Ostwald, M. 1965. "Pindar, *NOMOS* and Heracles (Pindar frg. 169 [Snell³] and *P.Oxy.* No. 1450, frg. 1)." *HSCP* 69:109–138.

——. 1969. *Nomos and the Beginning of the Athenian Democracy.* Oxford.

——. 1996. "Shares and Rights: Citizenship Greek Style and American Style." In Ober and Hedrick 1996:49–61.

Pagliaro, A. 1954. "Riflessi di etimologie iraniche nella tradizione storiographica greca." *Rendiconto dell'Accademia dei Lincei* s. VIII/9:134–153.

Parke, H. W., and D. E. W. Wormell. 1956. *The Delphic Oracle II: The Oracular Responses.* Oxford.

Payen, P. 1997. *Les îles nomades: Conquérir et résister dans l'enquête d'Hérodote.* Paris.

Pearson, L. 1939. *Early Ionian Historians.* Oxford.

Pedley, J. G. 1968. *Sardis in the Age of Croesus.* Norman.

Pelling, Christopher. 1997. "East is East and West is West—Or Are They? National Stereotypes in Herodotus." *Histos* 1. http://www.dur.ac.uk/Classics/histos/1997/pelling.html.

——. 2000. *Literary Texts and the Greek Historian.* London.

Peradotto, J. 1990. *Man in the Middle Voice.* Princeton.

——, et al., eds. 1993. *Bakhtin and Ancient Studies. Dialogues and Dialogics.* *Arethusa* 26/2. Baltimore.

Powell, A., ed. 1988. *Classical Sparta: Techniques Behind the Success.* Oklahoma Series in Classical Culture. London.

——. 1988a. "Mendacity and Sparta's Use of the Visual." In Powell 1988:173–192.

Powell, A., and S. Hodkinson, eds. 1994. *The Shadow of Sparta.* London and New York.

Powell, J. E. 1938. *A Lexicon to Herodotus.* Repr. Hildesheim 1950.

Prince, G. 1977. "Remarques sur les signes métanarratifs." *Degrés* 11/12:1–10.

Raaflaub, K. A. 1996. "Equalities and Inequalities in Athenian Democracy." In Ober and Hedrick 1996:139–174.

Rawlinson, G., trans. 1880[4]. *History of Herodotus.* 4 vols. New York.

Redfield, J. 1985. "Herodotus the Tourist." *CP* 80:97–118.

Roberts, J. T. 1996. "Athenian Equality: A Constant Surrounded by Flux." In Ober and Hedrick 1996:187–202.

Robinson, T. M. 1979. *Contrasting Arguments: An Edition of the Dissoi Logoi*. New York.

Rochette, B. 1995. "Les ξενικὰ et les βαρβαρικὰ ὀνόματα dans les théories linguistique gréco-latines." *AC* 65:91–105.

Romm, J. S. 1989. "Herodotus and Mythic Geography: The Case of the Hyperboreans." *TAPA* 119:97–117.

———. 1992. *The Edges of the Earth in Ancient Thought, Geography, Exploration and Fiction*. Princeton.

Rosellini, M., and S. Saïd. 1978. "Usages de femmes et autres nomoi chez les 'Sauvages' d'Hérodote." *ASNP* Ser 3.8:849–1005.

Rosen, R. M., and J. Farrell, eds. 1993. *Nomodeiktes. Greek Studies in Honor of Martin Ostwald*. Ann Arbor.

Rosivach, V. J. 1987. "Autochthony and the Athenians." *CQ* 37/2:294–306.

———. 1999. "Enslaving *Barbaroi* and the Athenian Ideology of Slavery." *Historia* 48/2:129–157.

Rotolo, V. 1972. "La comunicazione linguistica fra gli alloglotti nell'antichità classica." In *Studi classici in onore di Quintino Cataudella* I. 395–414. Catania.

Safire, W. 1999. "Holbrooke on Hold." *New York Times*, March 18, 1999:A25.

Saïd, E. W. 1978. *Orientalism*. London.

Saïd, S. 2002. "Greeks and Barbarians in Euripides' Tragedies: The End of Differences?" In Harrison 2002:62–100. [Trans. and repr. from *Ktema* 9 (1984) 27–53].

Salmon, A. 1956. "L'Experience de Psammétique (II.2)." *EC* 24:321–329.

Sebeok, Th. A., and E. Brody. 1979. "The Tongues of Croesus: A Myth about Communication in Herodotus." *QUCC* NS:7–22.

Sedley, D. E. 1998. "The Etymologies in Plato's Cratylus." *JHS* 118:140–154.

de Sanctis, G. 1933. "Intorno al razionalismo di Ecateo." *RFC* NS 11:5–15.

Schroeder, O. 1917. "Νόμος ὁ πάντων βασιλεύς." *Philologus* 74:195–204.

Schmitt, R. 1976. "The Medo-Persian Names of Herodotus in the Light of the New Evidence from Persepolis." *Acta Antiqua Academiae Scentiarum Hungaricae* 24:25–35.

Snowden, F. M. 1983. *Before Color Prejudice: The Ancient View of Blacks*. Cambridge, MA.

Sourvinou-Inwood, C. "Herodotus (and others) on Pelasgians: Some Perception of Ethnicity." In Derow and Parker 2003:103–144.

Spiegelberg, W. 1921. "Herodots Characteristik der ägyptischen Schrift." *Hermes* 56:434.

Stadter, P. 1992. "Herodotus and the Athenian *arche*." *ASNP* 22/3:781–809.

Stein, H. 1856–1908[6]. *Herodot*. Berlin.

Stier, H. E. 1928. "Νόμος βασιλεύς." *Philologus* 83:225–258.

Strauss Clay, J. 1972. "The *planktai* and *moly*: Divine Meaning in Homer." *Hermes* 100:127–131.

Sulzberger, M. 1926. "Ὄνομα ἐπώνυμον. Les noms propres chez Homère et dans la mythologie grecque." *REG* 39:385–447.

Svenbro, J. 1993. *Phrasikleia: An Anthropology of Reading Ancient Greece.* Trans. Janet Lloyd. Ithaca, NY and London. [Paris 1988].

Thissen, H. J. 1993. " 'αἰγυπτιάζων τῇ φωνῇ . . .': zum Umgang mit der ägyptischen Sprache in der griechisch-römischen Antike." *ZPE* 97:239–251.

Thomas, R. 1989. *Oral and Tradition and Written Record in Classical Athens.* Cambridge.

———. 1997. "Ethnography, Proof and Argument in Herodotus' *Histories*." *PCPS* 43:128–148.

———. 2000. *Herodotus in Context: Ethnography, Science and the Art of Persuasion.* Cambridge.

———. 2001. "Ethnicity, Genealogy, and Hellenism in Herodotus." In Malkin 2001:213–233.

Tuplin, C. 1999. "Greek Racism? Observations on the Character and Limits of Greek Ethnic Prejudice." In *Ancient Greeks West and East* (ed. G. R. Tsetskhladze) 47–75. Leiden.

Tyrrell, W. B. 1984. *Amazons: A Study in Athenian Mythmaking.* Baltimore and London.

Van der Veen, J. E. 1996. *The Significant and the Insignificant: Five Studies in Herodotus' View of History.* Amsterdam.

Vannicelli, P. 1997. "L'esperimento linguistico di Psammetico (Herodot. II 2): c'era una volta un frigio." In *Frigi e frigio*. Atti del 1° Simposio Internazionale, Roma 16–17 Ottobre 1995. Eds. R. Gusmani, M. Salvini and P. Vannicelli. Rome.

Vasunia, P. 2001. *The Gift of the Nile. Hellenizing Egypt from Aeschylus to Alexander.* Berkeley.

Vernant, J. P. 1981. "Le tyrant boiteux. D'Oidipe à Periandre." *Les temps de reflexion* 2:235–255.

———. 1989. "Food in the Countries of the Sun." In Detienne and Vernant 1989:64–169.

Walbank, F. W. 2002. "The Problem of Greek Nationality." In Harrison 2002:234–256. [Repr. from *Phoenix* 5:41–60 (1951)].

Watkins, C. 1970. "Language of Gods and Language of Men: Remarks on Some Indo-European Metalinguistic Traditions." In *Myth and Law Among the Indo-Europeans: Studies in Indo-European Comparative Mythology* (ed. J. Puhvel) 1970. Berkeley.

Weidner, E. 1913. "Βάρβαρος." *Glotta* 4:303–304.

Weiler, I. 1984. "Greek and Non-Greek World in the Archaic Period." *GRBS* 9/1:21–29.

Werner, J. 1989. "Kenntis und Bewertung fremder Sprachen bei den antiken Griechen I. Griechen und 'Barbaren': zum Sprachewusstsein und zum ethnische Bewusstsein in frühgriechischen Epos." *Philologus* 133:169–176.

West, S. 1985. "Herodotus's Epigraphical Interests." *CQ* 35:278–305.

———. 1988. "The Scythian Ultimatum (Herodotus IV 131, 132)." *JHS* 58:207–211.

———. 1991. "Herodotus' Portrait of Hecataeus." *JHS* 111:144–160.

Wolff, E. 1934. "Das geschlichte Verstehen in Tacitus Germania." *Hermes* 69:121–166.

Wood, H. 1972. *The Histories of Herodotus: An Analysis of the Formal Structure.* The Hague and Paris.

INDEX OF PASSAGES

Herodotus, Book 7 *(continued)*
75.1: 59
80: 31n8
83.1: 31n8
83.2: 59n131
85: 24
89.2: 30n2
94–95: 8n6
106–107: 57n118
114: 60n135
119: 61n140
125: 47n83
129.3: 42–43
134: 14n37, 62n142
135.1: 61n140
160.1: 17n50
161.3: 9n12
162.2: 17n50, 40n42
173.3: 16n46
180: 47n84, 60n135
188.3: 31n8
197.1–2: 60
204: 10n14
211.1: 31n8
224.1: 34n20
225: 47
226.1–2: 18n52
226.2: 17n50
228.6: 17n50
233.1: 22n16
Book 8
20.2: 59, 79
22.2: 71n14
34: 16n46
44.2: 41n50
52.1: 14n37
79.1: 47
131.2: 10n14
20.2: 2n10
43.3: 59
85.3: 53n106, 74n32
98.1–2: 53n106, 62–3, 63n144

99.2: 62n141
120: 59n127, 60n133
124.3: 14n37
133: 79
135: 2n7, 79
136–139: 16n46
141.1: 17
142–Book 9.11: 16–18
142.1–5: 16, 17n50.
144.2: 15–18
176.3: 14n37
188.2: 14n37
197.2: 14n37
Book 9
6: 16
7α.1–2: 16
9.1: 17n50
11.1–2: 16
11.2: 14n37, 17
11.3: 17
12.1: 62n142
16.2: 71n17
18.3: 57n118
20: 35
25.1: 12n28
26.2–4: 10n14
27: 10n14
32.1: 53n106
34.1: 40n42
39.1: 14n37, 56n115
43.3: 2n10, 70n11, 79
53.2: 17n50
61.3: 59n128
62.2: 59n128
76: 22n16
76.1: 59n131
79.1: 17n50
80.2: 60n133
82: 61n140
85.3: 41n47
90–91: 18n52
91: 47n84, 48

GENERAL INDEX

Underscored words are those identified as non-Greek by Herodotus

G

Gaia, 44–45

Garamantes, 25

Gela, 82

Geloni, 12n29, 24–25, 28n47, 34, 43

genos, 8 and n6

gerra (Persian wicker shields), 59

gestures, 22, 72–73

gloss, 5 and n26, 26
  of comparison, 24 and n24, 53,
    54n108, 63, 78
  ethnographic, 57 and n117, 60–62
  explanatory, 8
  of historie, 29 and n 50
  metalinguistic, 30–66, 82

glōssa ('tongue') 13–14, 21, 24 and
  n24, 25, 71, 80

goats, 19–21

Goetosyrus (Scythian name of
  Apollo), 31n5

Graces, 11n20

grammata ('letters'), 14n34, 26–27

Greek-barbarian antithesis, 1–2 and
  n9, 3, 8, 16–18, 45, 65–66, 72

Greek language. *See under* languages

Greek speakers, 2n7, 12 and n29, 13,
  27, 50

Greekness, 9–10

Gygadas ('Gygean gold'), 14n37

H

Hades, 31n5

harmamaxa (Persian chariot), 59

Hartog, F., 32

Hecataeus, 7–8, 41, 64

Hector, 45

Hegesistratos, 47n83, 48–49

Helen, 40

Hellēnikon, to ('Hellenicity'), 15, 18

Hellenization, 9n10, 9–10, 13

Hellespont, 9 and n10, 59

Hellespontiēs ('wind of the Hellespont'), 14n37

Hera, 11n20

Heraclids, 10, 15n43

hermēneis, 28, 74. *See also* interpreters

Hermes, 43 and n54. *See also* Mendes

Hermogenes, 42–43, 47

Hesiod, 11, 36, 38

Hestia, 11n20, 31n5

heteroglōssia, 1n3, 4, 29, 64

hippeis ('knights'), 14n37

hippobotai ('horse-riders'), 14n37

Histiaeus, 56, 71

histōr, 19
  Herodotus as, 4 and n19, 20, 28–
    29, 40, 43, 50, 52–53, 55, 62, 64,
    67, 77, 79, 82–83

historiē, 4n19, 26–29, 69n5, 73–74

historical narrative, 28, 52n103,
  56–63

Homer, 8n7, 11, 36, 38, 52–53, 71, 79

homoglōssoi ('speakers of the same
  language'), 16, 71

homonymy, 47n83

Horus (Egyptian name of Apollo) 11,
  31

hualos (Ethiopian glass), 53n106

'human generation,' 14n36

This book was composed by Ivy Livingston
and manufactured by Victor Graphics, Baltimore, MD

The typeface is Gentium, designed by Victor Gaultney
and distributed by SIL International